LEARNING DISABILITIES AND EARLY INTERVENTION STRATEGIES: HOW TO REFORM THE SPECIAL EDUCATION REFERRAL AND INDENTIFICATION PROCESS

United States Congress House of Representatives Committee on Education and the Workforce, Subcommittee on Education Reform

The BiblioGov Project is an effort to expand awareness of the public documents and records of the U.S. Government via print publications. In broadening the public understanding of government and its work, an enlightened democracy can grow and prosper. Ranging from historic Congressional Bills to the most recent Budget of the United States Government, the BiblioGov Project spans a wealth of government information. These works are now made available through an environmentally friendly, print-on-demand basis, using only what is necessary to meet the required demands of an interested public. We invite you to learn of the records of the U.S. Government, heightening the knowledge and debate that can lead from such publications.

Included are the following Collections:

Budget of The United States Government
Presidential Documents
United States Code
Education Reports from ERIC
GAO Reports
History of Bills
House Rules and Manual
Public and Private Laws
Code of Federal Regulations
Congressional Documents
Economic Indicators
Federal Register
Government Manuals
House Journal
Privacy act Issuances
Statutes at Large

LEARNING DISABILITIES AND EARLY INTERVENTION STRATEGIES: HOW TO REFORM THE SPECIAL EDUCATION REFERRAL AND IDENTIFICATION PROCESS

HEARING

BEFORE THE

SUBCOMMITTEE ON EDUCATION REFORM

OF THE

COMMITTEE ON EDUCATION AND THE WORKFORCE

HOUSE OF REPRESENTATIVES

ONE HUNDRED SEVENTH CONGRESS

SECOND SESSION

HEARING HELD IN WASHINGTON, DC, JUNE 6, 2002

Serial No. 107-65

Printed for the use of the Committee on Education and the Workforce

82-137 pdf

For sale by the Superintendent of Documents, U.S. Government Printing Office
Internet: bookstore.gpo.gov Phone: toll free (866) 512-1800; DC area (202) 512-1800
FAX: (202) 512-2250 Mail: Stop SSOP, Washington, DC 20402-0001

COMMITTEE ON EDUCATION AND THE WORKFORCE

JOHN A. BOEHNER, Ohio, *Chairman*

THOMAS E. PETRI, Wisconsin
MARGE ROUKEMA, New Jersey
CASS BALLENGER, North Carolina
PETER HOEKSTRA, Michigan
HOWARD P. "BUCK" McKEON, California
MICHAEL N. CASTLE, Delaware
SAM JOHNSON, Texas
JAMES C. GREENWOOD, Pennsylvania
LINDSEY O. GRAHAM, South Carolina
MARK E. SOUDER, Indiana
CHARLIE W. NORWOOD, JR., Georgia
BOB SCHAFFER, Colorado
FRED UPTON, Michigan
VAN HILLEARY, Tennessee
VERNON J. EHLERS, Michigan
THOMAS G. TANCREDO, Colorado
JIM DeMINT, South Carolina
JOHNNY ISAKSON, Georgia
BOB GOODLATTE, Virginia
JUDY BIGGERT, Illinois
TODD RUSSELL PLATTS, Pennsylvania
PATRICK J. TIBERI, Ohio
RIC KELLER, Florida
TOM OSBORNE, Nebraska
JOHN ABNEY CULBERSON, Texas
JOE WILSON, South Carolina

GEORGE MILLER, California
DALE E. KILDEE, Michigan
MAJOR R. OWENS, New York
DONALD M. PAYNE, New Jersey
PATSY MINK, Hawaii
ROBERT E. ANDREWS, New Jersey
TIM ROEMER, Indiana
ROBERT C. "BOBBY" SCOTT, Virginia
LYNN C. WOOLSEY, California
LYNN N. RIVERS, Michigan
RUBEN HINOJOSA, Texas
CAROLYN McCARTHY, New York
JOHN F. TIERNEY, Massachusetts
RON KIND, Wisconsin
LORETTA SANCHEZ, California
HAROLD E. FORD, JR., Tennessee
DENNIS KUCINICH, Ohio
DAVID WU, Oregon
RUSH D. HOLT, New Jersey
HILDA L. SOLIS, California
SUSAN DAVIS, California
BETTY McCOLLUM, Minnesota

Paula Nowakowski, Chief of Staff
John Lawrence, Minority Staff Director

SUBCOMMITTEE ON EDUCATION REFORM

MICHAEL N. CASTLE, Delaware, *Chairman*

BOB SCHAFFER, Colorado, *Vice Chairman*
THOMAS E. PETRI, Wisconsin
MARGE ROUKEMA, New Jersey
JAMES C. GREENWOOD, Pennsylvania
MARK E. SOUDER, Indiana
FRED UPTON, Michigan
VAN HILLEARY, Tennessee
VERNON J. EHLERS, Michigan
THOMAS G. TANCREDO, Colorado
JIM DeMINT, South Carolina
JUDY BIGGERT, Illinois
TODD RUSSELL PLATTS, Pennsylvania
RIC KELLER, Florida
TOM OSBORNE, Nebraska
JOHN ABNEY CULBERSON, Texas
JOE WILSON, South Carolina

DALE E. KILDEE, Michigan
ROBERT C. "BOBBY" SCOTT, Virginia
LYNN C. WOOLSEY, California
RUBEN HINOJOSA, Texas
CAROLYN McCARTHY, New York
LORETTA SANCHEZ, California
HAROLD E. FORD, Jr., Tennessee
HILDA L. SOLIS, California
SUSAN DAVIS, California
MAJOR R. OWENS, New York
DONALD M. PAYNE, New Jersey
TIM ROEMER, Indiana
RON KIND, Wisconsin
DENNIS J. KUCINICH, Ohio

TABLE OF CONTENTS

HEARING ON LEARNING DISABILITIES AND EARLY INTERVENTION STRATEGIES: HOW TO REFORM THE SPECIAL EDUCATION REFERRAL AND IDENTIFICATION PROCESS

THURSDAY, JUNE 6, 2002

U.S. HOUSE OF REPRESENTATIVES,

SUBCOMMITTEE ON EDUCATION REFORM,

COMMITTEE ON EDUCATION AND THE WORKFORCE,

WASHINGTON, D.C.

The subcommittee met, pursuant to notice, at 10:00 a.m., in Room 2175, Rayburn House Office Building, Hon. Michael Castle [chairman of the subcommittee] presiding.

Present: Representatives Castle, Ehlers, Platts, Osborne, Culberson, Wilson, Kildee, Scott, Woolsey, Solis, Davis, Owens, Payne, Roemer, and Kind.

Staff present: Kate Gorton, Professional Staff Member; Blake Hegeman, Legislative Assistant; Charles Hokanson, Professional Staff; Sally Lovejoy, Director of Education and Human Resources Policy; Patrick Lyden, Professional Staff Member; Deborah L. Samantar, Committee Clerk/Intern Coordinator; Bob Sweet, Professional Staff Member; Holli Traud, Legislative Assistant; Heather Valentine, Press Secretary; Liz Wheel, Legislative Assistant; Denise Forte, Minority Legislative Assistant/Education; Maggie McDow, Minority Legislative Assistant/Education; Alex Nock, Minority Legislative Assistant/Education; and Joe Novotny, Minority Staff Assistant/Education

Chairman Castle. The Subcommittee on Education Reform will come to order. We are meeting today to hear testimony on how to reform the special education referral and identification process. Under committee rule (b), opening statements are limited to the chairman and ranking minority member of the subcommittee. Therefore, if other members have statements, they may be included in the hearing record.

With that, I ask unanimous consent for the hearing record to remain open 14 days to allow member statements and other extraneous material referenced during the hearing to be submitted in the official hearing record. Without objection, so ordered.

OPENING STATEMENT OF CHAIRMAN MICHAEL CASTLE, SUBCOMMITTEE ON EDUCATION REFORM, COMMITTEE ON EDUCATION AND THE WORKFORCE, U.S. HOUSE OF REPRESENTATIVES, WASHINGTON, D.C.

Let me start by welcoming everybody here today. These hearings are continuing and are a matter of extraordinary importance. We appreciate the attendance of the Members of the House as well as, of course, our distinguished witnesses, who we will hear more about and more from shortly.

The Individuals with Disabilities Education Act, which is the federal education act that welcomes all learners and excludes none, regardless of their disabilities, is of extraordinary importance to this country. Today, children with disabilities sit with their non-disabled peers in regular classrooms and many learn from a general education curriculum. Yet, despite these significant accomplishments, children with disabilities are not completing school or performing at levels near their non-disabled peers.

As I have stated previously, it is not enough to open the schoolhouse door for children with special needs. We must ensure that we meet the letter as well as the spirit of the law and provide our children with the high-quality instruction and services they need to succeed. Just as we must move states and schools from simple compliance to real achievement, we must also ensure that our special education and general education programs evolve to meet the needs of a new generation of children with disabilities.

Today, more than half of our children in special education programs have specific learning disabilities. Yet, unlike some severe physical and mental disabilities, many children with learning disabilities are identified too late. Others are over-identified because they fail to learn fundamental skills like reading. In each case, frustration and an accumulated learning gap can spell disaster, with many children dropping out of high school and shunning higher education.

For these reasons, the purpose of this morning's hearing is to learn more about the way students with various learning disabilities are referred for special education-related services under IDEA. Specifically, I want to know if IDEA can be strengthened to prevent mild learning disabilities from turning into lifelong learning disabilities. I also want to know more about the models and strategies that have been effective in helping children learn in new ways. Finally, I believe it is important to hear more about effective, evidence-based early intervention programs and how they have been used to improve education outcomes. It is my hope that our distinguished witnesses will provide our members with a better understanding of each of these issues.

To that end, I am pleased to welcome a mentor and a friend, the former chairman of the Education and the Workforce Committee, Bill Goodling. Although I was sorry to see him retire to his farm in Seven Valleys, Pennsylvania, his counsel will carry me through IDEA reauthorization, just as it did with the reauthorization of ESEA.

I will proceed with the introduction of the rest of our distinguished panel in just a moment and Mr. Platts will do the introduction of Mr. Goodling.

First, I want to thank those of you in the audience as well as those listening to our IDEA hearing via live webcast. I know that many of you are interested in communicating directly with the Education and the Workforce Committee on issues related to learning disabilities as well as other topics in this series. To that end, my colleagues and I have unveiled a new interactive Great Ideas website on the Education and the Workforce Committee page. This will allow us to hear directly from the teachers and principals, parents and coaches, advocates and relatives who educate and care for our children with disabilities on the upcoming reform.

I know I speak for all our committee members when I encourage you to share your thoughts and reauthorization ideas. I look forward to hearing from you all.

Now, let's proceed with the hearing. First, of course, I yield to the distinguished ranking member, Mr. Kildee, for whatever opening statement he may wish to give. Dale?

WRITTEN OPENING STATEMENT OF CHAIRMAN MICHAEL CASTLE, SUBCOMMITTEE ON EDUCATION REFORM, COMMITTEE ON EDUCATION AND THE WORKFORCE, U.S. HOUSE OF REPRESENTATIVES, WASHINGTON, D.C. – SEE APPENDIX A

OPENING STATEMENT OF RANKING MINORITY MEMBER DALE E. KILDEE, SUBCOMMITTEE ON EDUCATION REFORM, COMMITTEE ON EDUCATION AND THE WORKFORCE, U.S. HOUSE OF REPRESENTATIVES, WASHINGTON, D.C.

Mr. Kildee. Thank you, Mr. Chairman. I am pleased to join Governor Castle at our latest hearing on reauthorization of IDEA. I want to join Governor Castle in welcoming our witnesses to today's hearing. I had a chance to meet with Secretary Pasternack yesterday, and I am certain the praise he has received by those in the field is indeed deserved. I also want to especially welcome my friend and former chairman of this committee, Bill Goodling. He has been my friend for many, many years, and will always be my friend.

During his career here in Congress and also as an educator, Bill Goodling worked hard to provide full funding for IDEA but also to improve the lives and education of children with disabilities. His appearance here today shows he maintains his commitment to our nation's children. Your leadership in the Congress on these issues is very much missed. I can recall back when you and I served on the Budget Committee many, many years ago. You and I offered an amendment on the budget for full funding for IDEA. And I got almost all my Democrats but you were the only Republican voting for that, and it took some courage to do that. And I always will remember that. You were a pioneer in this field, not a Johnny-come-lately.

Today's focus on learning disabilities, their identification, and the need for pre-referral behavior and academic intervention services is a crucial element of our review of IDEA. According to the Department's 23rd Annual Report to Congress, slightly less than half of all children with disabilities are identified as having learning disabilities. We must examine what services these children are being provided within IDEA and what interventions and supports can be provided prior to identification.

These interventions and support can make special education unnecessary for a number of children. However, some with identified learning disabilities will always need the protections and services provided under IDEA.

In any discussion of intervention services designed to reduce mis-identification, we must ensure that those services do not create barriers to those who need special education. Equally important in our discussion of intervention services is a need to have them address both academic and behavioral difficulties. A great deal of attention has been focused on children who struggle in reading. Intervention strategies must also address functional and behavioral problems that children experience.

Lastly, our efforts to examine the identification process and its impact on children must be done carefully. We need to continue to focus our efforts on full implementation of IDEA rather than seeking changes in the statute merely for the sake of change. This translates into a better technical assistance from the Department to states and from states to school districts. And this technical assistance is extremely important. In addition, it also demands a stronger enforcement role by the Department and possibly other agencies to target serious issues of non-compliance with the statute.

In closing, Mr. Chairman, I want to thank you for holding this hearing. I look forward to working with you on reauthorization in the coming months and next year.

Thank you, Mr. Chairman.

WRITTEN OPENING STATEMENT OF RANKING MINORITY MEMBER DALE E. KILDEE, SUBCOMMITTEE ON EDUCATION REFORM, COMMITTEE ON EDUCATION AND THE WORKFORCE, U.S. HOUSE OF REPRESENTATIVES, WASHINGTON, D.C. - SEE APPENDIX B

Chairman Castle. Thank you, Mr. Kildee. You probably heard the bells. We have a procedural vote on the floor. Because it is a procedural vote, sometimes there are other procedural votes; we aren't sure what is going to happen once we get there. I think the best way to proceed, because of the importance of the testimony of the first panel and the second panel, is to recess. Before we do that, I want to give an opportunity for the introductions of the witnesses. We will withhold their statements until after the vote is taken. The reason for that is there is a multitude of individuals who want to introduce Mr. Goodling. I don't know if they want to introduce him or just want to talk about him. And I want to let both Chairman Boehner and Mr. Platts, who succeeded Mr. Goodling, have that opportunity.

So let's proceed with that and see where we are time-wise after that. Chairman Boehner.

Mr. Boehner. Thank you, Mr. Chairman. I just want to welcome our good friend and my former mentor. He is someone who I pestered mightily when I was a junior member of this committee. Bill, we are glad that you are here. We know that you spent many decades in the classroom and many decades here in the Congress dealing with IDEA. We know that your testimony can be very helpful to us as we reauthorize the bill this year.

But for all of you in the audience, Mr. Goodling used to sit in that chair over there. Well, he used to sit in that chair where Mr. Kildee is sitting today. I used to sit way off in one of those corners and pester him. If Mr. Armey and I couldn't get Mr. Ford angry with us, we would get Mr. Goodling angry with us. If you are in a minority and you are a freshman, you didn't have much else to do.

But over the years, Bill and I have become very good friends. During my years in leadership and Bill's early years as chairman, we worked very closely together on a multitude of issues. I am just glad to see that you are here. Welcome.

Chairman Castle. Thank you, Chairman Boehner. As I indicated, Mr. Platts would like to also introduce his predecessor.

Mr. Platts. Thank you, Mr. Chairman. I am glad to add my words of welcome to Congressman Goodling. To echo the chairman's remarks, we certainly are sorry as a body and nation to have lost your expertise here in the committee and in the House. As one who succeeded you, I also have to say I am glad to have the opportunity to do so.

But I do want to herald that when Congressman Goodling stepped down, he was such a wonderful role model for all of us back home as a public servant. Twenty-six years here and for me a wonderful role model growing up as a constituent. But also 24 years as an educator. I think I have the years right that when he retired from the House, it was 50 years of public service in education, as an educator and in education as a Member of Congress. It is certainly an honor to be here and be serving, but a true and very distinct honor to be given the privilege of succeeding Congressman Goodling.

As I said to our current chairman, Chairman Boehner when I joined this committee, I share the desire, the commitment, and the interest in education. But I know it will take many, many, many years until I have even the chance to begin to fill in a small way the shoes of my predecessor, Congressman Goodling. It is wonderful to have you here, Bill. Thanks for your testimony today.

Chairman Castle. Thank you, Mr. Platts. We appreciate that introduction as well. I will resist the temptation to be the third one to introduce Chairman Goodling, except only to second the great comments we have had before.

What I am going to do is just go through Dr. Pasternack's background and then we will break for the members. We would encourage everybody to come back, because this is very significant testimony. Hopefully, it will be after one vote. We will go to the floor and try to figure out if that is what the situation is going to be.

Dr. Pasternack is the Assistant Secretary for Special Education and Rehabilitative Services at the U.S. Department of Education, where he serves as principal advisor to the Secretary on all issues regarding special education and the IDEA. He is also an ex officio member of the President's Commission on Excellence in Special Education. Previously, he served as state director of special education for the New Mexico State Department of Education. Dr. Pasternack holds a Ph.D. in special education from the University of New Mexico.

I have had an opportunity to meet with him. I overheard Mr. Kildee and Dr. Pasternack speaking and they have also had an opportunity to meet him. And, indeed, he is a gentleman who is as well versed in his field as anybody who has served in that position. We really appreciate him doing that, as well as his being here today.

So we appreciate both of you being here today. We will stand in brief recess to the call of the chair, which hopefully, will be as soon as we can get over and vote and get back if it is only one vote. We apologize for the inconvenience, but Chairman Goodling knows what it is all about.

We stand in recess.

[Recess.]

Chairman Castle. I think we are going to resume if we can.

Just so everybody knows, we may be in a series of odd votes and may have to break again at some point or continue the hearing with people going back and forth. Mr. Kildee should be back in a minute. But this is important. We want to move forward and get the testimony in. And with that, we will turn to a true star witness, the former chairman, Mr. William Goodling.

STATEMENT OF HON. WILLIAM F. GOODLING, FORMER CHAIRMAN, COMMITTEE ON EDUCATION AND THE WORKFORCE, WASHINGTON, D.C.

Mr. Goodling. Mr. Chairman, it is great to be back. What I miss most of all is my wonderful staff. To show you how bad it is, I went to one funeral a day late. I went to another memorial service a week early, because I don't have those pink cards in my pocket telling me where I am supposed to be every two seconds of the day.

I would hope that all of you would have time to read the statement. We put a lot of work into that, and I traveled throughout the country and talked to an awful lot of advocates, parents, teachers, and administrators. So I hope you will have time to read it. I am going to very quickly summarize what I think you should know.

I will start out simply by saying I would encourage you not to do massive surgery. I know you are going to get those who want you to do massive surgery and you are going to get those who want you to retreat on what we did in 1997. I suggest that you do neither. And I say that primarily because if you remember, the regulations did not come out for the first two years after the reauthorization. So the people back in the trenches are now just completing their second year of trying to implement what the regulations said they were to implement. So I encourage you not to give them a lot of new regulations on top of what they are presently trying to implement.

Secondly, I encourage you to move forward and complete the work that you have to do as quickly as you possibly can.

If you remember in 1996, we passed a program that we thought was filled with quality from one end to the other. We were trying to move the whole effort to have quality education for all of the children. The Senate did not act and in 1997 one of the most unbelievable things happened. We ended up with a bipartisan, bicameral, including a White House, proposal. It was overwhelmingly passed. It is the only time that ever happened in my 26 years. So I suggest that you let them implement that, because it would appear in my conversations around the country that some of the things that we were trying to do to improve the program are beginning to work.

I would like to very quickly summarize everything I have to say around the 40 percent phenomenon, because it has become the number one political issue. I can remember for the first 12 years, the only person I could get to help me talk about ``we have got to do something about this 40 percent'' was Congressman Kildee. Everybody else was talking about all the new programs have now. Forget about funding the last program. We have got to do the new things that are out there. Then Stennie Hoyer eventually came on board. In the last six years, it has become very politically popular to please those school board members back there, the school districts, and so on.

What I want to point out, however, is that 40 percent does not ensure a quality education for children with disabilities. It can, but it does not automatically. I don't know whether moving from the 6 percent during my six years as chairman to 13 or 14 percent has improved the quality dramatically or not.

Let me talk about how it can. If it is used properly, you could attract and keep quality teachers. The biggest problem we have at the present time in IDEA is attracting and keeping quality teachers. So that money could help you do that. It could help you do that several ways. First of all, paperwork is their greatest gripe and greatest complaint. If you are a teacher and you have to do an assessment and an IEP or a quality lesson plan for tomorrow's lesson, what are you going to do? Well, you are going to do the assessment and IEP. So you could use that money to help reduce that paperwork load. Now you can do that other ways. You could use it for increased technology to help reduce that paper load.

You could do it to train non-professional people. That is not the word I want to use. They are all professional. But if you could use it to have lay people trained, they could do a lot of that and you could keep some of those quality teachers and attract young people into the field.

You need to use that money also to make very sure that the regular classroom teacher gets the kind of training that they need in order to do their job. Many of the problems that are out there, including discipline problems, are due to the fact that the regular classroom teacher has had very little training and preparation. On average, there are four special needs youngsters in their class. You could use it effectively to do that.

You could use it to constantly upgrade the special education skills in general classroom teachers, because everything is changing. Right now, the physically and emotionally disabled, autistic, and all those programs are those, which there is not a great deal known about how you deal with the issue. So money could be used for that purpose.

If you use the money for early identification and diagnosis, you have to have trained people in order to diagnose those disabilities early. This would allow you to prevent an awful lot of over-identification and help an awful lot of young people. But people must be trained in order to notice that there is a problem. That has to be done early on. I guess I am saying Part C and Part D need all the help you can possibly give them in the program.

If we would use some of this money for quality early childhood family literacy programs, it would be a great help. If you had quality early childhood and family literacy programs, you could prevent an awful lot of young people from having the diagnosis. Now is not the time to reduce Even Start funding. Now is the time to increase Even Start funding. I just recently heard that a three-year-old child in an affluent home is equal to an adult's vocabulary in a home of poverty. So you see how important it is to deal with both the parent and the child.

We must also use some of this money to see whether we can find a way to keep some of it from going to litigation rather than helping children. I think you really need to take another look at that. The tragedy is that oftentimes teacher recommendations are ignored because the school district decides that it is too expensive to go on with this suit. So they just settle. That is a real challenge.

In summary, let me say that you have to look at the formula. I don't envy you, because I know how that is done. As soon as every member gets the printout, they look to see what they get. If they don't do well, then it is a bad formula. Forget about whether it was good for education or good for children. But you probably will have to look at it, because 40 percent could be 80 percent in some districts, in some states. It could be 20 percent in other states. So you will probably have to look at that.

Let me summarize simply by saying that this 40 percent phenomenon must translate into a quality program for all children. Funding and accountability must go hand in hand. Otherwise, you are not going to increase the opportunities for young children with disabilities to get a better education. Of course, that means your oversight responsibility is tremendous. Whether that will happen or not will depend primarily on your oversight ability.

Let me just close by reminding you of that picture up on the wall. The lips move all the time. And what do those lips say? They say, ``Quality, not quantity." They say, ``Results, not process." So you will hear that constantly as you are marking up the legislation.

Thank you for the opportunity to testify.

WRITTEN STATEMENT OF HON. WILLIAM F. GOODLING, FORMER CHAIRMAN, COMMITTEE ON EDUCATION AND THE WORKFORCE, WASHINGTON, D.C. – SEE APPENDIX C

Chairman Castle. Thank you, Chairman Goodling. Thank you for the warning about what we might hear from the lips up here as well. We really appreciate your being here. It is tremendous to have you.

Secretary Pasternack, we are also very interested in your testimony. You are next, sir.

STATEMENT OF ROBERT PASTERNACK, ASSISTANT SECRETARY FOR SPECIAL EDUCATION AND REHABILITATION SERVICES, U.S. DEPARTMENT OF EDUCATION, WASHINGTON, D.C.

Mr. Pasternack. Thank you, Mr. Chairman. It is a privilege to be here this morning. Thank you for the opportunity.

I would like to start by sharing with you that when Isaac Newton was asked how he had managed to see the world the way he did, he said it was because he stood on the shoulders of giants. That was how he was able to see the world as he did. So it is a privilege for me to be here this morning next to a giant, someone with a legacy of supporting kids with disabilities and their families. Thank you for allowing me the opportunity to be on the same panel with him.

It is also a great privilege for me to be testifying before you the same morning that you have invited my best friend and former college roommate, a guy that I actually taught in the same elementary school with. That is Reid Lyon. When we taught in the same elementary school, he taught third grade and I taught first grade. We both decided that neither one of us were trained very well on how to teach kids to read. Unfortunately, Mr. Chairman and members of the committee, I am sad to tell you that things haven't changed very much.

Part of the reason why I am here this morning is to talk about the fact that out of the 6.5 million kids with disabilities currently receiving special education, 2.8 million of those children are in one of our 13 categories of eligibility. That is the category of specific learning disability. Now, we know that there are seven types of learning disabilities. However, 80 to 90 percent of the kids in that category are there because they don't do one thing very well. That is they don't read. What we see is some problem differentiating those students who could learn to read if they were taught by highly qualified, well-trained personnel using scientifically based instructional practices.

Now, if those conditions existed in our public schools and if in fact teachers were being trained in how to do that, we think that we would see a significant difference in the kids who eventually displayed these kinds of intractable reading problems. We know that learning disabilities exist. There has been an incredible amount of very well done science to guide us in this area including converging science, neuro-imaging data, genetic data, and functional MRI data. That science is attributable to Dr. Lyon and his colleagues at NICHD. What we have learned from those longitudinal, multi-site studies of cohorts of kids is that there is a sub-group of kids who will not learn to read even when they are taught by highly qualified personnel using scientifically based instructional strategies. Those are kids who really do have disabilities. Those are kids that should be in special education.

However, from the studies that we have done at OSEP, we see that the kids currently in that category constitute a very heterogeneous group of kids. Part of that heterogeneity is due to the fact that the current regulations that are in place talk about a model of identifying kids with learning disabilities that has been in place since the mid-'70s. That model focuses on identifying a discrepancy between ability and achievement.

We think that we predict or identify ability by giving an IQ test. Right now, Mr. Chairman and members of the committee, there are about a million IQ tests a year given in this country. What we know from the work that has been done on IQ testing is that IQ tests don't predict much of anything. What they do is measure accumulated knowledge and don't help us identify a kid's ability.

What we would like to talk with you about and what we have been talking about in the testimony, we have heard across the country during the work that we have been doing the last six months on the President's Commission on Excellence in Special Education. I am proud to serve a President who thought enough about special education to create a presidential commission on Excellence in Special Education. We have heard no scientist that has come before us that supports the continuation of the IQ achievement model for identifying kids with learning disabilities. That is in fact a regulatory issue. One of the things that we hope to be talking with you and members of the committee about is the opportunity to change the statute to give us the ability to change the regulations, which focus on a practice that is fundamentally flawed and does not allow us to get the kids early.

Mr. Chairman, during the last 10 years we have seen about a 40 percent increase in the number of kids with learning disabilities that have been identified and placed in special education. The overwhelming majority of those kids are identified between the ages of 12 and 17 years of age. What we know from science is that that is too late. We have a model where we are waiting for kids to fail before we identify them as having a disability and placing them in special education. The best science available tells us that the earlier we identify these problems and the earlier we get to these kids, the higher the probability of successfully intervening and changing their life trajectory and helping them learn to read. If we continue a model where we are waiting for these kids to fail, then we are not doing what needs to be done.

So what I would submit to you is that the model that we have evolved, where we focus on a diagnosis for classification rather than diagnosis for instructional purposes, needs to be changed. As someone on the Commission said, ``It is time for us to drive a stake through the heart of the model that we have used to identify kids with learning disabilities in this country."

In closing, I would like to say that we know that learning disabilities exist. We know that they are real. We know that they are life-long. We know that their effect is pervasive. And we know that we have to go ahead and provide specially designed instruction to those kids who really do have learning disabilities. But the problem is we have kids in that category that really should not be in that category. The way to get them out of that category is to do what Dave Gordon has done at the Elk Grove schools. That is to teach kids how to read by having highly qualified teachers who get sustained, comprehensive, job-embedded professional development and use a scientifically based, proven, effective instructional model. Teach kids for two-and-a-half hours a day, K through 6, on how to read. What you will hear from him is that by doing that in Elk Grove, he went from 16 percent of his kids in special education to 9 percent of his kids in special education.

It is not about kicking kids out of special education. It is not about shutting down special education. It is about bringing the right kids into special education, kids who really have disabilities.

I look forward to the opportunity to respond to your questions and to continue to discuss this very important issue. Thank you for the opportunity to be here this morning.

WRITTEN STATEMENT OF ROBERT PASTERNACK, ASSISTANT SECRETARY FOR SPECIAL EDUCATION AND REHABILITATION SERVICES, U.S. DEPARTMENT OF EDUCATION, WASHINGTON, D.C. – SEE APPENDIX D

Chairman Castle. Thank you, Secretary Pasternack. Before I begin the five-minute questioning process by yielding to myself, I would just like to make a comment. In reading all of the testimony that I had available to me before the hearing today, I was struck by the intensity, knowledge, and desire of all of our witnesses today who want to make this system better. But also by the fact that they believe if we do not make adjustments to the system, it will not necessarily improve and that there are decisions that have to be made.

You obviously hit the one that stood out in everyone's testimony. That is reading, which is a very significant matter. I say that because in the past this has become strictly a funding issue. I think the funding issue is a significant and difficult issue, as Chairman Goodling pointed out. But the bottom line is that there is a lot more to be looked at besides funding that would advantage these young people and give them opportunities. I hope that everyone who is focused on IDEA this year will realize that we need to look at opportunities for improvements as well as the funding mechanism so that we can do exactly what Chairman Goodling mentioned that we did back in 1997 when we had a bipartisan, bicameral White House, congressional piece of legislation. Let's take the next steps beyond that. That was a heck of an improvement, but let's take the next step.

Let me yield to myself for five minutes of questioning. And let me start with Chairman Goodling, if I can. You discussed the funding formula for IDEA. Correct me if I don't say this quite accurately. My understanding of IDEA funding is that the federal role is to provide up to 40 percent of the funding. As you know, we did not do that. You have been, without a doubt in my mind, the strongest advocate for increasing the federal funding formula for many years. Only in recent years have we started to do this and have more than doubled it in terms of the percentage that we have increased it.

But I have always understood that essentially you are dealing with a whole pot of 100 percent. What we are doing is we are increasing the federal percentage of it, which reduces the need for the local and state government to make up the rest. However, it doesn't necessarily add more dollars to the overall funding for IDEA. In terms of improving it, is it your assumption that if money is freed up, some of that money would come back into IDEA as well as be freed up for other educational expenditures?

Mr. Goodling. Of course, any additional money that they receive in the local district means that they now have extra money to do whatever it is they want to do within the district. My concern is that one of those things is to help improve the quality of special education programs. I think that may not happen unless they hear that over and over and over again.

Now when you talk about C and D, which of course here you are talking about teacher training, you are talking about research. This is so important and I would hope those funds could be increased. I don't know how many years it has been since we have increased D money. If I understand the formula, and of course the formula experts are sitting up there, I tried to stay as far as I could from those. However, as I understand the formula, I believe that 40 percent - and, again, let me make sure we understand 40 percent of the average cost to educate a non-disabled child. At the present time if we do math easily, we will say that average is $7,000. So 40 percent is $2,800, and you should be spending $2,800 per child. Is that right, Sally? Okay, I checked with the experts here.

But I believe that that could send some states beyond that and some states below that. So it is something that I think you will have to look at. If you don't, I know what is going to happen. As the Members look at what they get, it becomes a real problem.

Chairman Castle. Actually, you have raised an interesting question, because it is important that we understand the formula. It is a little more complex than just 40 percent.

Mr. Goodling. It is very complex.

Chairman Castle. Let me turn to Secretary Pasternack for a moment. I was very interested in your statement as well and you are going to hear more about reading later today. I could not be in greater agreement with you. If we start to identify people as having learning disabilities when they are 12, you can almost forget it. Quite frankly, I think that if you start to identify them when they are five, you may have problems. I would be interested in your views on very early preparation. I don't want to call it necessarily education, but do you believe Head Start, daycare, the Federal Government, as well as the early reading money that has gone into the No Child Left Behind legislation from last year will make a difference? Are you looking at that? Are you in your role of worrying about special education, overseeing how this is being implemented as well as the connection between this and special education or removing children from special education?

Mr. Pasternack. Thanks for the question. I think one of the challenges to us is to use science and evidence to guide policy and infuse science into politics, which is your profession and not mine. Thank God. The opportunity that we have to do the right thing is difficult when you have so many people who are passionately clinging to their beliefs and their experiences and choose to ignore some of the evidence that is available. The evidence that we have is that the earlier we can get the kids, the higher the probability of successfully intervening in the lives of those kids.

You mentioned Head Start as an example. I think one of the things that we know from science is that the larger the number of letters that a child can identify before that child enters school is highly predictive of that child's future success in learning to read. Yet, students leave Head Start on average only identifying one letter of the alphabet according to the large-scale evaluative studies that have been done. What that suggests is that Head Start is a wonderful program and has done a great deal of good for lots of kids, but it is not rigorous enough in our view in terms of preparing students with the pre-academic skills that they need in order to benefit from instruction once they enter kindergarten.

You mentioned Early Childhood. One of the responsibilities that I have is to chair the Federal Interagency Coordinating Council. This council is supposed to advise nine cabinet agencies on early childhood issues, particularly early childhood issues affecting kids with disabilities. Our hope is that by integrating services and collaborating across agencies, we can prevent kids from developing the conditions. This makes it difficult for them to benefit from education once they enter public school. There is an incredible opportunity there for us if we work with daycare programs and if we build family literacy skills. We know, for example, that lap time, a child - when I was talking with Congressman Kildee about his grandkids the other day, he was telling me about reading to them.

Well, I read to my grandkids as well. I think many of us as parents read to our kids. If you can't read, then you can't read to your children. We know this from well-done research that just an opportunity to sit on the lap of a parent and hear the parent read is incredibly helpful to kids learning language. And that language learning is helping them prepare to learn to read.

So to the question that you asked about Reading First and Early Reading First, I applaud the bipartisan, bicameral approach to the most fundamental education reform that we have seen in the last 35 years. We hope that those programs will significantly improve reading acquisition for all kids.

Mr. Chairman, 40 percent of kids are going to learn to read despite what we do to them when they go to school. Our challenge is to focus on the other kids who are at risk of having difficulty learning to read. Now we know that direct, systematic instruction will help most of those kids to read. But the 2 to 6 percent of the total school population that have intractable reading problems are the kids that we are really struggling to identify the right kinds of strategies. I am sad to say that 27 years into the implementation of this law, we still haven't identified the most effective instructional practices to be able to use with that small group of kids that really do have disabilities and really do have these intractable, persistent reading problems.

But what I can tell you is that giving them IQ tests and trying to identify this discrepancy between ability and achievement will not improve our ability to instruct these kids. It is about providing high-quality, scientifically based instruction, which will give them the kind of reading skills that we need them to have to be able to benefit from future instruction down the road.

Chairman Castle. I appreciate that. As you sat there and told us the story of reading to the child, I worry about the children whose parents cannot read at all. That is a comment, not a question, because I am going to turn to Mr. Scott for the next round of questioning. There are a lot of societal concerns that we are going to have to undertake in order to prevent the problems that exist.

Mr. Scott?

Mr. Scott. Thank you, Mr. Chairman. And I want to thank our witnesses. Comment has been made about how this passed last time on a bipartisan basis. That would not have been possible without the leadership from this committee. IDEA can often be very controversial. And, it took strong leadership to get everybody together. And, Mr. Goodling, I want to thank you for providing that leadership.

Secretary Pasternack, if you don't use the IQ tests, what should you use?

Mr. Pasternack. Thank you, Mr. Scott. We believe we should actually be using a problem-solving approach where you would have three tiers of the identification process. The first tier would be you use the--since we are talking about reading, and since 80 and 90 percent of the kids in the LD category have problems in reading, I will just confine my response to the reading problem. There is a basal approach to teaching reading. However, some kids don't benefit from that approach. Those kids would then go to the second tier, which includes programs like Title I and Title VII. These are the supplemental programs that are available through the fine work that Congress has done in creating those programs.

Then you have some kids who don't even benefit from that level of intervention. Those are the kids who would get the kind of assessment that we would be talking about, which is really just an assessment of their reading deficits. Then based on assessing their reading deficits, one could begin to decide that a kid needs special education. The assessments would then help the teachers to develop an instructional model, which would allow them to help teach the kid how to read.

So it is a problem-solving model. It is currently in use in the state of Idaho where as a state they basically said we don't need to use an IQ achievement discrepancy model to identify kids with learning disabilities. Interestingly enough, the percentage of kids with learning disabilities has remained pretty much the same in that state. But they are convinced that the kinds of kids they are identifying are really kids who do have learning disabilities and they are able to spend their money differently. Rather than wasting it on unnecessary assessments, they are able to use assessments that can help teachers identify the instructional needs of kids rather than talking about whether a kid have an IQ of 80 or 90 or 100.

Mr. Scott. Well, after you have gone through that evaluation process, how do you differentiate between someone who has a deficit because of a learning disability and someone who has a deficit because they were just subjected to a bad educational process?

Mr. Pasternack. The most important decision that needs to be made is documenting failure to respond to scientifically base instructional practices delivered by highly qualified personnel. When you have that kind of documentation, you can be convinced that the kid you are looking at really does have an intractable reading problem, a specific learning disability in the area of reading. Then people can make the second tier of that decision, which determines whether that student needs specially designed instruction provided through special education.

Mr. Scott. Now does all this evaluation process take so long as to violate your principle of providing the services as early as possible?

Mr. Pasternack. That is a great question. I would hope not. I think right now we are seeing school psychologists who aren't able to help. They are spending too much of their time attending meetings and providing what has been described as a legal inoculation. This is where districts are so worried about failing to comply with the process parts of the regulations that the school psychologists don't have the opportunity to actually administer the kinds of tests that they have been trained to administer in helping implement these problem-solving models and doing things like functional behavioral assessments and developing positive behavior intervention plans instead of spending.

For example, I was in Palm Beach and they have got 70 school psychologists. When I asked them what they spent the majority of their time doing, they said they spend most of it going to meetings. As a school psychologist, I don't believe that is what I was trained to do. I was trained to help kids. I think many school psychologists and many special-ed teachers that Chairman Goodling alluded to are frustrated by the fact that they are spending too much of their time filling out paperwork and going to meetings and therefore they don't have time to actually provide high quality instruction.

Mr. Scott. I think we are hearing results of a process -

Mr. Pasternack. You are sure hearing it from me.

Mr. Scott. - in what you just said. If we use more of Part C, could we reduce the need for Part B services?

Mr. Pasternack. Absolutely.

Mr. Scott. Good. What can we do to increase the service - we do all this evaluation, what can we do to increase the quality of services that are provided. You mentioned training. You also mentioned Iowa. In terms of suspensions, there is one study in Iowa that was done where they showed they came in with services to the teachers, showing them best practices where they reduced the number of suspensions from something in the hundreds to a handful. What should we be doing to increase the quality of services after you have evaluated someone?

Mr. Pasternack. No matter what we do in statute, no matter what we do in regulation, and no matter what we do in funding, if we don't have highly-qualified personnel teaching our kids, we are never going to get to the improved results that the President is demanding and that the Congress has the right to expect and that parents want to see.

As an example, I am frustrated by the fact that when you go out and talk to teachers around the country, they don't know about something as fundamentally important as progress monitoring. This is where you sit with a kid and you ask that kid in one minute to read to you and you count how many words that kid correctly reads in a one-minute probe. This doesn't require technology, it requires the equipment that you have in your hand, which is a pencil and a piece of paper. It is not an expensive approach and yet we don't have teachers who are trained on how to do that.

I believe that we have to work with our colleagues in higher ed to find out why they are not training teachers differently based on the science that is available now that wasn't available 10 years ago. When I was trained, I wasn't trained on how to teach kids how to read. I believe I was guilty of malpractice back then and I believe many of our teachers want to do the right thing. They are not malicious in trying to deny kids free and appropriate public education; they just don't have the skills.

So I believe it is about pre-service preparation. And it is about high-quality, comprehensive, sustained job-embedded professional development.

Mr. Scott. Thank you, Mr. Chairman.

Chairman Castle. Thank you, Mr. Scott.

Mr. Wilson?

Mr. Wilson. I was very interested in your concern about paperwork. You indicated interest in providing more modern technology to assist the teachers in preparing the IEPs. Are there any efforts being made to reduce the size of the IEPs or to simplify them in addition to use of technology?

Mr. Goodling. What I see happening out there, as I ask people, ``Where did that regulation come from?" is the state, trying to make very sure that they are complying with whatever the Federal Government wants. They pour it on. Then the local district adds additional regulations in order to make sure that they are following the line that they are supposed to follow.

Yes, if we could assure the state and the local district that you are meeting those regulations and they are simple enough to understand, then I think you could reduce that paperwork.

But, again, I think you could solve an awful lot of these problems if you could have para-professionals properly trained to help and if you could have teachers, both in the regular classroom, properly trained to deal with the issue.

That is why I said C and D money is extremely important, because you are talking about research. You are talking about teacher training. You are talking about re-training.

So in answer to your question, yes, I think it could be reduced dramatically. I think it has to be reduced dramatically, because these people are leaving the profession because they want to teach. Young people are not coming into the profession because they have heard of all of these horror stories about how teachers have to spend all their time on assessments, IEPS, and so on. As a result, they don't have time to prepare a decent lesson.

Mr. Pasternack. Mr. Wilson, as we move forward, I hope that we can talk about the fact that right now we have a system that cares more about who is in an IEP rather than what is on an IEP. There aren't enough trees in America to keep slaughtering them at the rate that we are slaughtering them in the name of providing specially designed instruction to kids with disabilities.

We have to make this process simpler, and we have to focus on a model where we ask four fundamental questions: Where is the kid now? Where is he going to get to? How are you going to get him there? And how are you going to know when the kid gets there? That is what an IEP should be about. But instead you have people whose fear of a lawsuit is driving the kinds of discussions and the kinds of decisions that they are making rather than focusing on providing a high-quality program to kids that is designed to provide measurable results. And then we just need to go about measuring the results.

Chairman Goodling is exactly right. We are losing competent, qualified, and dedicated people in alarming numbers because they are spending too much of their time going to meetings and filling out paperwork. We did a national study that documents that sad fact.

Mr. Wilson. I do understand it from two angles. My wife is a teacher. I have also had the opportunity to meet with educators for my children for IEPs and it has worked out beautifully. It is just that I thought I was educated. Then I was overwhelmed with the minutia of what I thought was in the IEP. In fact, I was really intrigued by your pointing out the four points. It seems to me that would have been sufficient. I didn't need to know how to make a watch. Indeed, I, again, thought I was fairly educated until I was overwhelmed with more information than I ever wanted to know, understand, or comprehend.

And so I really look forward to efforts at simplification for educators and for parents.

I have no further questions.

Chairman Castle. Thank you, Mr. Wilson.

Mr. Owens.

Mr. Owens. Mr. Chairman, I am pleased to welcome our former chairman back and I am glad to hear that he is looking over our shoulders. We certainly want to make certain that we follow through on some of the commitments that were made. And the 40 percent to IDEA is one of those commitments that is long overdue.

I just want to start by asking you to clarify a little confusion there before about how the formula works. Is it appropriate to assume that the 40 percent of whatever is being expended would be met and the money freed up from a local education agency can be used somewhere else for local education so that everybody gains regardless of whether everybody gets the same, is that correct?

Mr. Goodling. Yes, I think you have to look at the formula simply because, as I understand the formulas, one state could be getting 60 or 70 percent. Another state might be getting 30 percent as you move toward ``full funding."

But it is very important that that money is freeing up an awful lot of demands that the local school district has for all of their students. But when they get that money, they shouldn't forget that improving the quality of a special education program is very, very important.

And then, as I also said, increase C and D so that you can really do some of the things that have to be done in order to improve the education for all children.

Mr. Owens. Is it correct to assume that that 40 percent is kind of open-ended; it is like an entitlement, right?

Mr. Goodling. Pardon?

Mr. Owens. The 40 percent promised by the Federal Government is kind of open-ended, it doesn't have a cap on it, right?

Mr. Goodling. Well, when the program started, it wasn't a mandate. No one was mandated to participate in the federal special education program. You would have been a fool not to take the federal dollars, because the courts were going to make sure you were doing what you should be doing for children with disabilities. But it was not a mandate. The 40 percent was all confused, because what was in Senate language was that Congress would strive to get to 40 percent of the average cost to educate a non-special ed student. As I said earlier, the average cost today is something like $7,000. So 40 percent of that is $2,800.

So you would be as the Federal Government sending $2,800 back for each student that was in special education. That is why I always said not to focus on over-identification, because of the money. The $2,800 is not going to get them very far, because the cost may be 10 times as great for an individual student.

But I think you have to look at the formula. I can just see everybody up here. They will look at the print outs and ask how their district or state did. I think you could get a discrepancy in relationship to the 40 percent due to the way the different formulas are set up at the present time.

Mr. Owens. But even the $2,800 hypothetical figure would be on a per pupil basis. So the number of pupils would determine ultimately the amount of money that the local education agency would receive?

Mr. Goodling. Today, you should be sending $2,800 per pupil back to the state, per pupil who is in IDEA.

Mr. Owens. Now, you mentioned over-identification and the major problem in a large urban area like New York City where I have parents in revolt against special education because they feel too great a number of their youngsters are being routed to special education as an easy answer to a discipline problem, a behavior problem, maybe a slight emotional problem, and the figures keep growing. And I understand from some study that was done, it is not just New York City, that it is a problem all over.

In your perspective now, having backed away from things a bit, do you have any ideas about how we could work with that problem a little more? I once proposed an amendment whereby we have a transition period to allow funding for a transition program to come out of the special education funds for discipline problems in youngsters who might have been misidentified so that we would transition out of this problem of over-identification and hopefully one day establish programs that are designed to deal with behavior problems and deal with them separately as behavior problems. Either one of you that might have - Mr. Pasternack, you might have an answer to that problem, too.

Mr. Goodling. In outlining what I thought could happen if you got to 40 percent - early identification is just so important for these young people - and programs, if you remember, I constantly told the Members that Head Start early on was not giving these children a head start at all. Every study that was done told us that. Title I was not giving children an opportunity to improve their academic achievement at all, and every study showed us that. I kept harping on the fact that we have got to talk in terms of quality, quality, quality in those programs. That is why, of course, I am harping today on C and D, because the research, the preparation of teachers, the preparation of those who identify, helping teachers and administrators deal better with parents are very important if we are going to improve the quality of education for those with disabilities.

What I cautioned was don't get carried away with the 40 percent as a political argument. Make sure that we are talking about quality, quality, quality for the children that we are trying to help.

Mr. Pasternack. Congressman Owens, I was just in Brooklyn on Saturday talking to a group of parents of kids with disabilities, and I have great empathy for Chancellor Levy in trying to serve a district with 1.2 million students in it. I know that he faces great challenges.

The issue that you raise about kids with behavior problems is very complicated. Head Start around the country has reported that the number one increase in requests for technical assistance is about young kids between the ages of 3 and 5 years of age with behavior problems. I think one of the things that we are seeing, particularly in school age kids with behavior problems, is that the reason that they have behavior problems is because they fail to learn how to read. That frustration leads them to both act out and act inwardly. One of the things that I am concerned about is the fact that we have done a much better job acting out kids that we call externalizers. These are the kids who act out and who are easily identified, and we haven't done as good a job identifying the kids who withdraw and are depressed and become kids who refuse to go to school and are at higher risk for suicide and things like that.

We see many kids who enter the juvenile justice system because of their failure to succeed in school. An interesting statistic, very quickly, is that there is more juvenile crime committed during the school year than during the summer. One would speculate that there would be more juvenile crime committed during the summer, because of idle hands being linked to doing the devil's work. But the hypothesis that underlies that is that the kids are frustrated by their lack of success in school during the school year. That is one of the reasons why they commit some of the acts that they do.

I think that we should free up some of the school psychologists and the people who provide related services in schools to provide some help to the very difficult issue that you raise. They should be identifying why these kids are having behavior problems and developing programs to help intervene with the behavior problems that these kids are having, rather than focusing on the administration of tests.

Mr. Goodling. May I just add that I have been telling the administration over and over again to avoid focusing on every child reading at the third grade level at the end of third grade. Instead, focus on every child reading at the first grade level at the end of first grade. If they are not reading at the first grade level at the end of first grade, I can assure you that millions will not be reading at the third grade level at the end of third grade. They will not read at the first grade level at the end of first grade unless they have a quality family literacy program prior to that for millions of children. As the Secretary has said over and over again, we can reduce identification for IDEA dramatically if we can deal with that reading problem.

Chairman Castle. Thank you, Mr. Owens.

Mr. Goodling. Reading readiness problem.

Chairman Castle. I will now yield to Ms. Woolsey for five minutes. I would like to point out that we are reacquainting her with her favorite chairman. I don't remember the two of them ever disagreeing about anything in the whole time they were together.

[Laughter.]

Ms. Woolsey. We didn't disagree, did we, Mr. Chairman?

Mr. Goodling. Thank you for the letter.

Ms. Woolsey. You are welcome. Thank you for dropping by my office. You are wearing your retirement well, and it is nice to have you back here.

Now, I wasn't here, I am sorry, for your testimony, but I am going to assume you talked about funding for IDEA and you talked about quality educators. So I want to ask you a question about funding. We have finally put some more money through appropriations into the states for IDEA, not 40 percent. But what I am finding in my state of California that our governor has taken that increase and put it some place else. Well, I mean he has put it in IDEA and then taken that amount they were putting into it and moved it to some place else in education or to some place else in the state budget. So instead of supplementing with the increase, they are supplanting. And we are going to be reauthorizing, and I would suggest you could help us maybe with some language that would make that not possible for states. What good is it for us to reach 40 percent and then have them not use it?

Mr. Goodling. As I indicated both in my testimony and in answer to some questions, if you do not do an outstanding oversight job, my greatest fear is that the 40 percent will be a political accomplishment and make an awful lot of people feel good back in districts. It will do nothing to improve the education of children with disabilities.

So you are going to have to be very, very vigilant. If they get that additional money, that frees them up from using all sorts of money that they would have for other purposes. They should concentrate on how could they improve the quality of education for the disabled. That is the purpose of the money.

Ms. Woolsey. And that is the purpose of the money.

Mr. Goodling. This is why I said you are going to have to be very careful for your formula.

Ms. Woolsey. Well, both of you, I am sure you - in your testimony, you have given us lots of good ideas and I certainly know you have a lot of good ideas, Mr. Chairman. Are there bad ideas that are being kicked around that we should be aware of before we reauthorize?

Mr. Goodling. What I had said in my initial statement was that I would be very careful that -

Ms. Woolsey. You keep reminding me that I was not here for that. You are always nagging at me.

Mr. Goodling. I had said in my initial statement that you have to be very careful in my estimation that you don't do massive surgery. We did that in 1996 and 1997. The regulations were delayed a couple of years before they were ever published. Therefore, you have states and school districts just in their second year of implementation.

As I travel the country, it appears that some of the things that we were trying to do to improve the quality of the program are working. But they are just in the business of getting those regulations down the way they should be. So I cautioned against giving them a lot of new regulations or you will have them going through this same process all over again and it won't result necessarily in quality education for disabled children.

Ms. Woolsey. Mr. Pasternack?

Mr. Goodling. So fine tune, I am saying.

Ms. Woolsey. Fine-tune but not operate.

Mr. Goodling. There needs to be some fine-tuning.

Mr. Pasternack. I think that one of the bad ideas is to do nothing to the IDEA and leave it in its current form. In my view and from what I hear from practitioners, parents, and kids, we have got to go ahead and make the law simpler. It has gotten way too complicated.

A bad idea is to continue focusing on process and not to change our focus to accountability for results. A bad idea is not to put any more money into it. I am proud to serve a President that asked for the largest single presidentially requested increase in IDEA funding in history.

I think there are bad ideas about not using the science and the evidence that we have to guide policy and inform us on how we make this change in order to focus more on results and accountability for those results rather than policy, procedure, and more regulation.

It is an interesting question. No one has ever asked a question like that. That is a very interesting way to pose a question. And that would be an initial response. I would like to think about that some more.

Mr. Goodling. It would be a bad idea not to increase funding dramatically in C and D.

Ms. Woolsey. Okay, thank you very much.

Mr. Pasternack. Amen.

Ms. Woolsey. Thank you, Mr. Chairman.

Chairman Castle. Thank you, Ms. Woolsey. On the issue of C and D, just for everyone's edification, it is my understanding that the C program is for the younger program. I think the D program is for research. This is basically funding which is outside of the formula, is that correct? Just to underline what it is that we are saying about the formula and the C and D references we have here today.

Mr. Pasternack. C is for our program that serves infants and toddlers, birth through 2 years of age. Part D funds things like research, as you mentioned, personnel preparation, our parent training and information centers, which is a critically important service that we provide, and some other related programs.

Chairman Castle. They are not part of the B formula, which goes back to the schools for the children with disabilities, is that correct?

Mr. Pasternack. That is correct, Mr. Chairman. Those are our discretionary dollars as opposed to the formula dollars.

Mr. Goodling could not be more right in saying that we have got to invest more in those things in order to improve results under Part B.

Chairman Castle. Well, I am going to resist the temptation to have a second round of questioning here, because we have another panel. However, it is a temptation. This has been very enlightening. We very much appreciate your testimony here today. We also know you are both individuals with busy schedules, and we appreciate your taking the time to join us. Obviously, we welcome Chairman Goodling back at any time for his reunion with everybody here.

So we thank you.

Mr. Goodling. And you can demand that the Secretary come back.

Chairman Castle. Oh, that is correct. Or we can subpoena if worst comes to worst. No, thank you. We really appreciate it.

Mr. Pasternack. Thank you, Mr. Chairman.

Chairman Castle. Why don't we formulate the second panel. We may try to keep this rolling, because we are going to start to lose time. So if the next group could gather at the table, we will start the hearing. Somebody may take over for me when I go to vote, and we will keep it going that way.

Let me introduce the three witnesses. The first is Dr. G. Reid Lyon. Dr. Reid Lyon is a research psychologist and the chief of the Child Development and Behavior Branch of the National Institute of Child Health and Human Development. He serves as an ex officio member of the President's Commission on Excellence in Special Education. Prior to joining the NIH, he served as a faculty member at Northwestern University and the University of Vermont. He holds a Ph.D. from the University of New Mexico with a dual concentration in psychology and development disabilities.

I might say he is well named. We have begun to ``lionize'' quite a few things around here. We discussed what he has done in his department when we did OERI. I was at a discussion recently in which your name came up again in terms of duplicating how you have done things. So we appreciate all you have done and look forward to hearing from you today.

Our second witness in this particular group will be Dr. Joe Kovaleski, who is the Director of Pupil Services at Cornwall-Lebanon School District in Lebanon, Pennsylvania. He previously served as a director of research and evaluation for the instructional support system of Pennsylvania. Dr. Kovaleski currently serves as a member of the editorial board of School Psychology Review and is a member of the National Association of School Psychologists Cadre on IDEA. He holds a Doctor of Education degree from Penn State.

Mr. David W. Gordon is the superintendent of the Elk Grove Unified School District in Elk Grove, California and serves as a member of the President's Commission on Excellence in Special Education. Prior to assuming his current position, he served as assistant superintendent of elementary education for Elk Grove Unified. He holds a Master of Education degree in educational administration from Harvard University.

We appreciate all of you being here. What we are going to do is start this, Dr. Lyon. If somebody comes back to replace me, we will continue it. If not, we will have to break to go from there. We expect somebody to return shortly.

So, Dr. Reid Lyon.

STATEMENT OF G. REID LYON, RESEARCH PSYCHOLOGIST AND CHIEF, CHILD DEVELOPMENT AND BEHAVIOR BRANCH, NATIONAL INSTITUTE OF CHILD HEALTH AND HUMAN DEVELOPMENT, ROCKVILLE, MARYLAND

Mr. Lyon. Thank you, Chairman Castle. And thank you for the kind remarks. It is an honor to be here and an honor to follow the two previous witnesses. As you know, Chairman Goodling was a champion of infusing science into educational practice and policy. It was delightful to see him. Representative Ehlers is not here, but he also was a strong advocate for making sure that what we do with children is supported and informed by the best science we have available. And to you, sir, for that equal emphasis on making sure that what we use with children has been shown to work.

It is easy for me to make this testimony this morning, because I can summarize only what has been already said. I don't need to take us down other paths other than to say that we can do much better with children who have learning disabilities by putting in place that which has been discussed already.

We know that many of the youngsters who are now identified as learning disabled are in fact mis-identified, primarily because they haven't been taught effectively in classroom situations. That means that the amount of instruction that has to be provided to all of the children in LD is diffused, diluted, and not being given to those children who most effectively need it.

That occurs for a variety of reasons that have already been mentioned. Learning disabilities and kids with learning disabilities are typically identified at older ages. The largest influx of youngsters coming into the system are 11 to 17 years of age. The reason for that is that we now have in place a set of criteria, which requires that kids manifest an IQ achievement discrepancy, a gap between two psychometric measures. That gap typically does not show itself until the kid is about 9 to 10 years of age. By that time, the youngster has already failed for two, three, four, or five years. Motivation to learn is very minimal.

Secondly, we have youngsters going into both special education and classroom settings where the teachers have not been prepared, as Secretary Pasternack indicated, to address the tremendous variability in how these youngsters come to the classroom. Many of the kids do have bonafide genuine learning disabilities, but many have come from environments which have not provided the background language and literacy information. This puts them behind the curve once they come into kindergarten, first, second, and third grades. When they get there, we don't have the instructional capability to meet their individual needs.

So there are two issues here. First, we are mis-identifying youngsters at a very late stage, because of incorrect psychometric measures and procedures. Secondly, we are identifying children much too late. Thirdly, even if we were to identify them earlier, much of our teaching force has not been provided with the critical information they need to address individual differences in kids.

And, fourthly, we are not holding schools and the system accountable for making sure what we do works. I cannot say it any better than Dr. Pasternack said, our job is to make sure we identify the right children, that we bring to bear the best evidence-based instruction as early as possible, and that we make sure that it has actually had an effect.

If I could, I will depart from the way that I usually speak with you all and take you through some data, but very child-centered data. On page 14 of the testimony, you are going to find a series of bar graphs. Let me take you through what that means. What you can see, if you have that in front of you, is a graph labeled first grade. And the years noted are 1995 through 1999. If you will note above each bar, there is a figure. That denotes the percentage of kids within that population who are identified as at risk or already failing in reading.

This is a school system. These data are derived from a school system in one of NICHD studies where we knew there was a high rate of reading failure. We could predict that on the basis of many things but mostly these kids are poor. Sixty percent of them are on free and reduced lunch and 60 percent of them come from minority families. Many of those families have parents who cannot read themselves.

Before we start the project, what you are looking at is this astounding number of kids who cannot read; 31.8 percent of first graders at the end of that first grade year still cannot read. Between those two years, we brought to bear a research program that put in place early identification in kindergarten. That brought to bear comprehensive instruction for teachers in terms of what it takes for kids to learn how to read, how you assess reading development, and how you address what you get from the assessment with good instructional strategies.

It is an evolving process. This shows how long it takes to bring evidence-based practices, early identification, and early intervention into schools. It has a demonstrable effect.

In 1995, again, 31.8 percent of the children could not read at the end of the first grade year. In 1996, we had reduced that to 20.4 percent of the children. As we became more adept at providing early intervention and early identification services and scientifically based instruction in 1997, the percentage of kids at the end of the first grade year drops to 10.9. As you can see, in 1999, only 3.7 percent of those kids at the end of the first grade year have difficulties reading.

It is that 3.9 percent of the children who we believe are bona fide, genuine learning disabled students that we now have to bring to bear more research and intensive study to determine how we can in fact deal with these refractory or recalcitrant reading problems.

But that is a very strong indication of when we can put in place what we know how to do; we can actually save the educational lives of all of these children. And then focus our resources on those that need the more intensive instruction.

While the Members' figure that looks like this doesn't show up in color, although the chairman has one in color, let me show you that when we teach well, we also do pretty good brain surgery. If you look, Mr. Chairman and Mr. Kind, you can see this is also in front of you. On the right-hand side of that figure, you will notice a left hemisphere of the human brain. We can determine within brains at these early ages whether or not the neural systems that work hard to read are working well.

If you look at the top right-hand picture, you will see a very small display of red color. That color just indicates to us the degree of physiologic activation in those systems that are handling reading. You will note in the top right-hand side that is a fairly minuscule amount of activation. At the end of this first grade intervention period, if you will look down below, we not only had demonstrable increases in reading behavior to the average level in both word reading skills and comprehension, but also notice how the brain has indeed changed and has normalized.

When teachers get the kids early, when they identify early what it is that are putting kids at risk and they bring to bear strong evidence-based instruction, we cannot only move those kids, the majority of kids to average or above average levels of reading, but in fact we can make sure that physiologically they are becoming more healthy as well.

I would like to stop there and would be delighted to answer any questions as we move along.

WRITTEN STATEMENT OF G. REID LYON, RESEARCH PSYCHOLOGIST AND CHIEF, CHILD DEVELOPMENT AND BEHAVIOR BRANCH, NATIONAL INSTITUTE OF CHILD HEALTH AND HUMAN DEVELOPMENT, ROCKVILLE, MARYLAND – SEE APPENDIX E

Mr. Platts. [presiding] Thank you, Dr. Lyon. We are going to reserve questions until the end of when all the panelists are done speaking, but thanks for your testimony. I do have some follow-up for you on the graphs you just referenced.

Dr. Kovaleski, thanks for being with us and especially as a fellow central Pennsylvanian.

STATEMENT OF JOSEPH F. KOVALESKI, DIRECTOR OF PUPIL SERVICES, CORNWALL-LEBANON SCHOOL DISTRICT, LITITZ, PENNSYLVANIA

Mr. Kovaleski. Thank you. And thank you to all of the members of the committee for this invitation. I am delighted to be here. I reflected as I was waiting this morning that I started my graduate program in 1975, which was the year that IDEA was drafted first as PL-94-142, and started practicing as a school psychologist in 1977, which was the year of the regulations. So I have seen this law grow up as I have grown up professionally.

And the interesting thing about that is the issues that we are addressing today about the special education identification process have been around since that time. I can say that early on in my career, we were over-identifying too many kids in this area. I have also seen at the same time an overwhelming of the special education system by having too many students in the system.

What happens in regular education is also interesting because when students have been identified in large numbers as learning disabled, regular education has come to believe it has a very limited capability of providing service for students and a limited ability to do that for students. What happens then is the teachers come for any kind of problem that they see in kids and start looking for disabilities rather than thinking about good instruction.

Luckily for me, in your introduction for me, you did not say what was probably the most important job I had in my career. Between 1990 and 1997, I was director of the instructional support team process in Pennsylvania, which was a statewide program that was targeted toward addressing these issues in terms of improving regular education and also stopping the growth in special education by not having these students need special education.

The process that we used was called an instructional support team and we implemented the process in over 1,700 schools during that period in all 500 school districts in Pennsylvania. The program provides a building-based approach to helping teachers by providing curriculum-based assessment and other procedures where we can identify exactly what students need and provide services just in time when they need it. In-class support was an important part of this program. And what we tried to do during that process was to identify the student's rate of learning and a lot of talk today about the discrepancy. I think one thing we have to look at is not only how discrepant kids are, but also their rate of learning in the face of appropriate instruction.

When we implemented this program in those 1,700 schools, we found that 85 percent of the kids that were identified for the process did not need a further individual evaluation for special education. This was 1990 to 1997 and before we had Dr. Lyon's research. So just having that process in place we were able to cut off referrals for special education and the need for special education dramatically.

From that experience as well as talking to colleagues from across the country that have used similar models of pre-referral intervention teams, I want to offer the following recommendations or conclusions.

First of all, referrals for special education eligibility screening can be greatly reduced by using an effective pre-referral intervention program. We know that there are a large number of students who can learn if support interventions are delivered before the problems develop and before learned helplessness sets in.

Secondly, the testing process itself, as it is typically implemented, leads to mis-identification. Typically, what happens in most schools that don't have this kind of early intervention pre-referral process use what is called the Refer Test Place Program. Basically, you refer students to the school psychologist. Then you identify whether or not they qualify based on various formulas and you go from there. That process itself leads to over-identification. Or what I might rather say is mis-identification because what you get oftentimes from teachers at the school level is not only that we have too many kids in special education, we have the wrong kids in special education and we have the wrong kids identified for learning disabilities. I would be happy to go into that more in detail during the question and answer period if you would like.

Based on our experience with these teams, we found that the best way to identify the right kids for special education is to use what Dr. Pasternack referred to as the response to intervention process. We can identify a student's rate of learning when provided with effective instruction. And what we have found is the best way to identify which kids are the right kids is to see which kids who fail to make progress in spite of our best and most scientifically-based efforts.

There also needs to be a fully funded early literacy program that provides intensive intervention for students who are at risk for not learning to read by the third grade. We know which kids need intervention by kindergarten or first grade. We have appropriate assessment procedures that can identify which kids need intervention. What we don't know is which of those kids are eligible for special education. So that leads me to my next point. There needs to be a coordination of the various federal programs: special education, remedial education, Title I, and general education so that we can address effective intervention programs. We don't need to identify kids as learning disabled at kindergarten or first grade. In fact, that is a really bad idea. What we need to do is provide intensive intervention and help schools understand how they can use all of the services that they have in a more coordinated way.

Teachers of administrative service and related service personnel address students' needs best when they are organized in teams. We found that the instructional support team process in Pennsylvania not only helped to support teachers individually by allowing them to address the needs of individual kids, but it really helped the whole school to watch and monitor everybody so that we knew who was falling through the cracks and who was falling behind so that we could deliver just-in-time services to the kids who needed it most.

As we heard earlier this morning, we also think that the screening and early identification process needs to identify students' emotional and behavioral needs as early as possible. As a school psychologist, we know that during our experience with ISTs and also on a day-to-day basis many of the problems that we get are about social and emotional issues. We need to keep that front and center as we address the issues that we are talking about today.

In summary, we have talked about these issues now for decades, since I entered the field. I think we are at the point where the research that has been talked about earlier has caught up to the rhetoric and I think we need to look at the recommendations that I have included today. I think what they would help us with is they would help to improve general education. We can't think about this process as a special education issue. Special ed does not sit out there somewhere separately. It is inherently connected to the general education program. We need to improve general education in order to prevent students from needing special education.

I also think that the recommendations I have been talking about today would help prevent those problems and reserve special education for those students who truly need it.

I thank you for the opportunity to address this group and would be happy to answer your questions.

WRITTEN STATEMENT OF JOSEPH F. KOVALESKI, DIRECTOR OF PUPIL SERVICES, CORNWALL-LEBANON SCHOOL DISTRICT, LITITZ, PENNSYLVANIA – SEE APPENDIX F

Mr. Platts. Thank you, Dr. Kovaleski. We will come back to questions after Mr. Gordon.

Mr. Gordon?

STATEMENT OF DAVID W. GORDON, SUPERINTENDENT, ELK GROVE UNIFIED SCHOOL DISTRICT, ELK GROVE, CALIFORNIA

Mr. Gordon. Thank you, Chairman and Members, for the invitation.

I certainly concur with what has been said before, number one, that we have got to throw out the IQ testing as a means of identifying students. Secondly, we are over-identifying children in my state and in this nation, and I would like to tell you my district's story of what happened.

My district is a 50,000-student district in the southern part of Sacramento County, California. We project to grow to 80,000 children in the next eight years. We serve a wonderfully diverse population. Thirty percent of our students are white. Sixty-three percent are children of color. Our students also speak more than 80 languages and dialects.

When I came to Elk Grove almost 11 years ago, I was in charge of elementary education and was shocked to find out that 16 percent of the students in the district were in special education, 16 percent. And what was going on is we were waiting until the discrepancy got large enough to refer the children to special ed and they were going in and never getting out.

So what we decided to do is go before our state board of education and ask for a waiver to be able to use our special ed money in kindergarten, first, and second grade, because the teachers at those levels could tell you with great precision which kids you would identify three years later. So we began serving those kids with a very focused instructional strategy based on the kind of teamwork that Mr. Kovaleski described.

All of our instructional people work together. There are no empires and fiefdoms. The Title I people team with the general education and special education people try to catch the reading problems as early as possible.

Now, what has been the result? Well, the result is that in the last 11 years, our special ed population has dropped from 16 percent to just under 9 percent. So we are now confident that we are serving the right children. In addition to that, we have a good relationship with our parents. Our IEP processes go smoothly. We have not had a due process hearing in the 11 years that I have been in the school district.

So I think my recommendation to you is much like Dr. Kovaleski's. We have got to get our programs working together. We are also wasting a lot of money because we allow these services to operate in isolation, and we have got to somehow find some ways to make IDEA work better with the ESEA and with the general education program. I also think we have to add some more accountability for results in special education. We should not be bashful about saying we want to assess every special education student in a competent, quality way, and let's give some feedback to parents based on the results.

Thank you.

WRITTEN STATEMENT OF DAVID W. GORDON, SUPERINTENDENT, ELK GROVE UNIFIED SCHOOL DISTRICT, ELK GROVE, CALIFORNIA – SEE APPENDIX G

Chairman Castle. Thank you very much, Mr. Gordon. I apologize for missing all of your testimony. As a matter of fact, we are trying to see if somebody else wants to start the questioning first for that reason.

Mr. Platts, are you prepared to go ahead so I can get caught up? Mr. Platts, I yield to you for five minutes.

Mr. Platts. Thank you, Mr. Chairman. Again, I thank all of you for your testimony.

Dr. Lyon, when you were sharing your numbers, there was certainly a dramatic reduction in first graders not being able to read. I want to make sure that I am reading your graphs right; the top and bottom graphs represent first graders who were 31.8, when they were second graders, 14.5. Was that the same group?

Mr. Lyon. No, sir. No, it is not.

Mr. Platts. Okay.

Mr. Lyon. The top graph is just the first grades, each first grade that year.

Mr. Platts. Okay.

Mr. Lyon. Lets say you are in the first grade in 1995 and you are part of that bigger group. I am in the first grade in 1996. That is my graph. Then another first grade comes behind us the next year. These are not the same kids over time. This is the effect of putting teacher preparation and the early identification and intervention in place as well as integrating special and regular education in a cohesive manner to address the needs. The bottom graph shows in 1996 that as we get better with doing it with first graders, obviously, second graders now begin to benefit from our increased knowledge and so forth.

So the second great cohort that came in 1996, 14.5 of them were still disabled readers, but we had learned over the next several years enough to make sure that cohort coming in 1999 was 2.4 percent.

Mr. Platts. But it is the same school, right?

Mr. Lyon. The same school.

Mr. Platts. So 1995's first graders are 1996's second graders?

Mr. Lyon. No - yes, that is correct.

Mr. Platts. So we had almost a 20 percent drop?

Mr. Lyon. That is correct.

Mr. Platts. That improved from first to second grade, so we can correlate it out?

Mr. Lyon. Right. It is important to not just look at the data but to look at the conditions that have to be in place to ensure these changes can actually happen. Both my fellow witnesses from the public school systems have realized this for years. You cannot implement even the best research-based programs without preparing the system to do so. Even the best preparation will take time. We have to make sure that our teachers have the support and the preparation to understand both the assessment and teaching side of things. Number two, we have to make sure that it is not just a special education issue, but rather it is a general education/special education collaborative. In fact, at the Hartsfield School, all instruction takes place within the classroom, with the special educator and the classroom teacher working together, but grouping students to focus that instruction.

At the same time, the most powerful instructional time for kids is in the morning. All of the instructional time has been moved to that time of the day and extended so kids get more time to learn and practice.

Because the IQ achievement discrepancy model had been replaced by early intervention models, we have to make sure that the parents of these children understand at every step of the way what we are trying to do. You have got to, and I think everybody does recognize, that the existing IDEA and its regulations, with its process, heavy process requirements and its heavy regulatory requirements, is frankly there because parents are very fearful that the system will not take care of their children. That is, IDEA is focused not on education as much as protection.

Now, when we want to be able to bring to bear the best science we have, that informs instruction better than it ever has, and we have converging evidence from multiple sites that says we can do it, we still must make sure that all unintended consequences of these changes are taken into account. We must also study how to actually implement this type of information to make it effective and don't randomly throw these programs in when our teachers are not trained, when our systems are not ready, and when are principals are not ready to go.

Mr. Platts. I appreciate that important point. It has got to be that comprehensive team approach and everyone on the same page to make it work.

In my few remaining seconds, I am going to say quickly to Dr. Kovaleski, I appreciate your testimony. Would you be able to quickly touch on two things? First, you said not only are too many students over-identified, but the wrong students are in special ed. Could you expand on that and then on the instructional support team? While I was in the statehouse for eight years in Pennsylvania, we unfortunately cut back the state support and made it more of a local option. If you want to comment on that, that would be great.

Mr. Kovaleski. Sure. Just to give you a kind of graphic example, and I don't have graphs so I will have to use my hands. If you imagine two kids that both have what we call standard scores of 70 and that is they are way behind in just looking at the discrepancy model. Let's imagine one of those students has average intelligence and the other student has intelligence that is more commensurate with their achievement. The way people think about the learning disability identification process now is that the student who has - now both of these kids both have a hard time learning, we do our best to teach them and they have a difficulty learning. The student with the high IQ under the current system qualifies as eligible for special education. The other student whose IQ is more commensurate with what they are achieving does not qualify. There are a lot of people that believe that those students do not need special education.

What I have said many times about this is that what people are in effect saying is that the second student is not smart enough to be in special education. That is an absurdity and it happens all the time in this country. What we really need to be about is not looking at who is discrepant from what. Instead, we need to look at who is having the most difficulty learning when provided with very effective, scientifically based instruction.

We have procedures that we have used for years based on curriculum-based measures, for example, and we have literary graphed data to see students' progress over time. I think we are able to identify the best kids.

In terms of what happened in Pennsylvania with IST, it was set in as a state mandate in 1990 and de-regulated in about 1998. I am happy to report that most districts that I talk to have institutionalized this as a procedure. However, as with anyone, you need to maintain a high degree of special development support for processes like that. Otherwise, the new people that come on do not implement it as well as anything. Anything we are talking about today really needs to be implemented with a high degree of fidelity in order to work.

Mr. Platts. Thank you again for your testimony.

Thank you, Mr. Chairman.

Chairman Castle. Thank you, Mr. Platts.

Mr. Kildee?

Mr. Kildee. Thank you very much, Mr. Chairman. I apologize for being absent for a while but I had to be on the floor for a foreign policy debate.

Let me first ask Dr. Lyon, I certainly agree with the need to provide early intervention for children. However, your testimony also mentions the fact that many older children have been identified as being learning disabled. What can we do to give them meaningful help when they are identified later, possibly by the general education teacher? And how important is good contact between the general education teacher and the special education teacher?

Mr. Lyon. Thank you for the question, Mr. Kildee. Since you were in the well when I was introduced, I want to thank you again, since you didn't hear it, for yours, Mr. Castle's and Mr. Ehlers' emphasis on making sure that sciences drives instruction as much as possible. I believe it has been that leadership along with ex-Chairman Goodling that has allowed us to come some steps in answering this question.

Older kids have a tough time. Whether they are learning disabled or not, kids who are not achieving after the third grade have already suffered multiple years of failure. We have learned as we follow thousands of these kids that even if we bring good strong instruction to some of them, they resist it. They resist it, because they no longer have the motivation to look stupid, which they think they will do.

So in answering your question, we have had to be extraordinarily creative in trying to understand how we can bring to bear instruction in reading, writing and mathematics with older kids when they are failing that does not make them look dumb, but goes back and builds all the foundational knowledge that has not been in place and provides them with a level of success so they keep going.

There are two solutions to that. The first is again the black hole we are trying to fill in teacher preparation. This means making sure that teachers know how reading develops, what goes wrong, and what you do about it at every age. Consider that most kids after third grade are now confronted with learning content, social science, history, literature, and so forth. If you can't read, that is pretty rough. So we have to make sure that we have content-area teachers that have an understanding, not so much the specialty but an understanding of how the kids are dealing with that content that is above their level. Then they must learn how they should collaborate and communicate with specialized instructional personnel and special educators to present the information in a readable way.

Still when we do that, we find tremendous resistance in older kids. Both the NIH and OCEF are working to provide youngsters with these difficulties with digitized kinds of textual information in the content area. OCEF has done a great job of this by bringing history, science, and mathematics texts to the kids by allowing the kids to push on words that they don't know and the book talks to them. As they are helping the kids read through, and this can be done more privately, the book asks them questions about what they are reading in the content area. So it will ask them specific questions about the science concept they just have read about or the social studies concept. This is a type of technology that is interactive. It helps to build motivation. It can be done, again, within the integrity of the kids' lives so they are not being embarrassed and so forth.

We have to make sure of another thing with older kids. As they are struggling in reading and we are bringing to bear better instruction and technology to help them, we have to be able to continue to get them the information in alternative ways. We have to provide accommodations, whether that means books on tape or whether that is whatever it takes to get around the disability.

Mr. Kildee. In kindergarten through third grade, basically, a child learns to read and after that they read to learn. So if they have not learned to read by the third grade, maybe because of some special learning disability, there is a socialization problem that has to be addressed then, too, does it not?

Mr. Lyon. Absolutely. Again, as Secretary Pasternack testified, the biggest predictor of poor self-concept, behavioral difficulties later on, difficulties adjusting to life, and getting a good job or not a good job, is this ability to learn through print. If you don't do it, we have a lot of downstream consequences.

But, again, I think by putting in place what we are recommending today, the number of kids that actually have these difficulties, which now ranges from 5 to 20 percent in some states, will reduce down to 6 percent or less. The data that I have shown this morning and the data that Dr. Gordon is talking about indicates that when we can bring those numbers down of those children who did not respond to the powerful instruction, we can now focus much more intensively on what to do. But to be sure, we have a lot to learn about how in fact we will help that 2 to 6 percent come around in reading. Every example I gave you in response to your question is in a sense a prophylaxis. That is, we are not actually changing reading behavior yet. We still have 2 to 6 percent of our kids, who with the best instruction, are slow, inaccurate readers and hate to do it. We have got to figure that out.

Mr. Kildee. Thank you very much for your response and for your testimony, and thank you for everything you are doing.

Chairman Castle. Thank you, Mr. Kildee. Mr. Ehlers?

Mr. Ehlers. Thank you, Mr. Chairman. I apologize that I missed some of the discussion, because we had to go vote. I hope I am not going over old ground. First of all, just to comment, Dr. Lyon, in response to your comments. As I am sure you are aware, instruction in math and science also helps children learn how to read. But it also struck me once. Years ago when I was still teaching, I took a group of students into a school and they each taught four students on science. I remember a group of four youngsters coming in and the teacher pulled me aside and said this one person is very slow, treat him gently. It turned out he was the best of the four, because he had never before experienced someone trying to teach him science properly. Obviously, he had skills that had not been recognized in the school.

I just wanted to ask, based on your background, Dr. Lyon, how accurately and scientifically can we characterize learning disabilities and what types of categories can we set up? Secondly, have we yet learned what instruction works best with what category?

And let me give you a specific example. I have a grandson who is very dyslexic and so I have learned a lot about dyslexia. The standard methods of teaching never helped him. My daughter put him into private school for dyslexics and he is finally in high school and is learning how to read. It really struck me that nowhere along the line did someone really identify him well and teach him properly for his disability. Are there other cases like this? How many categories are there and is it possible for a school system to have the resources to address the needs of each category?

Mr. Lyon. A good question, a tough question, a complex question. Let me see if I can address it with clarity. In IDEA there are currently seven major types of learning disabilities. You can have a learning disability in listening, speaking, basic reading skills, which mean the word level skills, reading comprehension, mathematics calculation, mathematics reasoning, and written expression. Now, obviously, kids can come with one, all of those, or subsets of those. As has been testified to this morning, the largest majority of kids within that larger umbrella are youngsters who have problems in basic reading skills. Eighty to 90 percent of all of the youngsters have difficulties there.

As you pointed out, difficulties in reading portend difficulties in science and mathematics and any other content area where you have to bring the information in through print. So quite a few kids are going to be in classrooms that have multiple difficulties. As you know, we know the most about reading. We have placed a great deal of emphasis understanding reading, because it is the most prevalent. It is the foundational ability for everything that comes after. For some reason, it is more highly related to the kid's self-esteem, self-concept, and occupational success later on, even more than science. I hate to say that, but even more than science.

Mr. Ehlers. I agree.

Mr. Lyon. The fact is when we bring to bear our converging evidence; we have a very good idea of why difficulties in learning to read occur and the different sub-types that exist. Through your efforts in helping us bring science to this process, we have been able to identify what it takes to learn to read. We know kids have to have the underlying sound structure well developed. They have to have phonics, no matter how controversial that is. They have to be able to apply the sound structure in phonics to print rapidly and accurately. They have to have good vocabularies to understand what they read. And they have to bring to bear active strategies to comprehend.

We have good measures of all of those components of reading. And we have good measures that can give us an idea of who is going to have a tough time at 5 and 6 six years of age. We are moving down to 3 and 4 now under the new Early Reading First initiatives and so forth.

Through the efforts of this committee in promoting this kind of work and clinical trials, we also now understand which teaching approaches are most beneficial for which children or different types of difficulties in reading. It is through these efforts that we can get to all but about 6 percent of the kids. Within that 6 percent, those children that we would consider dyslexic or learning-disabled in reading, we are making tremendous strides and bringing that down to 5 and 3 and 2 percent in some of our studies.

What goes into the instruction is extremely well known. It is the intensity, consistency, and the preparation of the teacher delivering that intense and consistent instruction. We know the components of the instruction, and we also know that general educators can apply these kinds of procedures as well to kids who may or may not be disabled and actually bring about tremendous change.

So we are getting very good at it. The difficulty, as we have always talked before, is infusing what we know into practice. That is a much more complex issue that requires bolstering teacher preparation, having leadership as to my left that can bring the information into schools, and making sure teachers understand and can apply it.

Mr. Ehlers. Just one last quick question. When you classify the students, is there some good scientific basis for it or does it end up being largely the judgment of a practitioner?

Mr. Lyon. At the present time, it is highly subjective, highly variable, and, frankly, the identification process is based upon invalid concepts. I hate to continue to drive the stake into this discrepancy point, but using an IQ achievement discrepancy to identify someone with learning disabilities does not make any sense because it does not differentiate the disability.

For purposes of example, let me do it this way. I am going to get into trouble, but let's say on this side of Chairman Castle are people with high IQ's.

Chairman Castle. You are already in trouble now.

Mr. Lyon. Yes, sir.

Chairman Castle. I can tell you right now.

Mr. Lyon. In the context of that high IQ, there is underachievement in reading or math. There is a discrepancy. I am on this side. Just for today, we have lower IQ scores, just for today. The only reason I put us on this side is I know you and so you will bear with me. They have a discrepancy and we don't have a discrepancy. If the discrepancy had any value to it, they would respond to instruction differently than we would. They would have different physiology from us. Their development course would look differently from us. None of those differences can be obtained. The discrepancy does nothing to differentiate what it takes to learn to read, how one responds to instruction, and what the developmental outcomes look like.

So why do you keep it? We keep it, because it has been put in place for a long time. People can actually derive discrepancies through testing very well. I mean they know how to do this extremely well. One of the things I have noticed over the years that we have been working at is that people will continue to do what they know how to do extremely well irrespective of whether or not it affects children positively.

Mr. Ehlers. So, in other words, it is bad but we don't know of anything better?

Mr. Lyon. We do know of a lot better. We actually can look at kids in terms of their achievement, their reading, their math, their writing, and their language. We can then look at the achievement and determine whether or not they respond to instruction. Using those two variables, we then begin to identify the learning disability from that context.

Chairman Castle. Thank you, Mr. Ehlers.

Mr. Scott?

Mr. Scott. Thank you, Mr. Chairman. I wanted to somewhat follow up on that same line of questions. On your chart, Dr. Lyon, what portion of the fewer people being identified was due to better testing and how much of it was due to the fact that - this is the end of the first grade, right, after you have actually provided some instruction, how much of it was better instruction and how much of it was better evaluation?

Mr. Lyon. The two are hand in hand, Mr. Scott. Obviously, we are identifying at the end of the first grade reading achievement levels. Frequently, that is not done. What we are looking at in 1995 in the top bar is the traditional instruction and evaluation procedures being employed and resulting in this very high rate of reading failure. That is, it is identified after the fact. Between 1995 and 1996, both kindergarten and first grade early screenings were put in place and the instructional procedures necessary to attempt to alleviate the difficulties were also put in place. We are dropping to 20.4 in the second cohort of first graders, primarily as a function of now improved early assessment and improved teaching.

Keep in mind it is a process. The school, the system, and the teachers are learning how to do it better. In 1997, a new group of first graders come in. There has been improvement not really on the assessment side, but now on the instructional side in integrating classroom and special education in the classroom.

So what you are seeing is the growth curve within a school that takes place when the early assessment is put in place and the instructional procedures that we know that work are also put in place. The fact that it takes five years, at least in this school, to get to a 3.7 failure rate from a 31.8 failure rate in first grade cohorts is the amount of time it has taken to implement these processes well.

Mr. Scott. It is interesting that people are doing this much better because the instruction is better. That is one of the concerns some of us have about this every year testing. The old adage, you don't fatten the pig by weighing the pig. If you are not actually improving the instruction, all you are doing is punishing the children. Here you got - it wasn't the children's fault that they weren't learning, it was the system that they were subjected to.

Mr. Lyon. Yes, and I think that is a very articulate way to put it. These are system casualties. These are instructional casualties in the main. I think as both of the experts on my left have mentioned, when you are trying to bring to bear special instruction, special education with this large group, many of whom are instructional casualties, you can't focus effectively on those who need the more specialized help. You are diffusing and diluting the process.

Mr. Scott. Did any of this improvement come about because of better use of Part C?

Mr. Lyon. Absolutely, absolutely.

Mr. Scott. I notice in one chart I saw a couple of hundred thousand are getting Part C benefits and millions are getting Part B benefits. As we reauthorize, maybe we ought to focus a little bit more attention on Part C funding.

Mr. Lyon. Yes, sir.

Mr. Scott. Mr. Kovaleski, in your testimony, you indicated a need to test emotional needs as well as academic needs. Could you elaborate on that?

Mr. Kovaleski. I think I wouldn't characterize it as ``test." I think to be sensitive to and identify - frankly, emotional and behavioral needs in school are pretty easy to identify. Teachers will tell you very quickly who needs help in that area.

I agree with Dr. Pasternack's earlier testimony that a large part of that is frustration over not being able to read. The other part of it that we do have to realize is that there are kids coming from all kind of environments that frankly didn't exist when you and I went to school or if they did, they existed in much smaller numbers. Those are not just impoverished environments or environments that fail to produce vocabulary, but they are also harmful to kids.

Mr. Scott. How does all that translate into something we can do something about?

Mr. Kovaleski. You didn't ask me that. The question is do we need to be sensitive to that? I think we have to be ready to provide effective interventions early in all areas, not only academic but also emotional support and behavioral support. It is not a testing issue. It is very much an issue where we can provide strong programs for kids.

Mr. Scott. Did you want to comment on that, Mr. Gordon?

Mr. Gordon. I was just going to say one thing we are starting to do in our Title I schools, we have re-configured the funding and we are putting in a person we are calling a behavior intervention specialist. This is not a counselor, but someone who will work with the principal and the teachers to work through issues with kids. Again, trying to start that as early as possible. But we are just starting it now and we are hoping to find enough money to do it in all our schools.

Chairman Castle. Thank you, Mr. Scott.

Mr. Wilson?

Mr. Wilson. Thank you, Mr. Chairman. Dr. Kovaleski, I was very interested in your observation about over-identification. Then I was equally interested in the ISTs and how you described in-class support for the instructional support teams. Can you go a little bit further in layman's terms and describe how this system works?

Mr. Kovaleski. By looking at group data in schools, we identify who is falling between the cracks. At that point, we have a team of people that work with the classroom teacher to what we call systematically search for what works. Part of that is to use good assessment systems to identify where the discrepancies are academically and/or behaviorally, and then to help teachers.

One of the things we have talked about a lot of today that I agree with is the issue of teacher preparation. It is not going to be very soon that we have teachers that are absolutely prepared for every type of student with a difficulty in school. What we found through instructional support is by having support teachers, school psychologists, guidance counselors, remedial teachers actually go into classrooms with teachers and try to figure out how to help students by assessing them effectively and then providing good strategies, it is the best staff development program that we have ever seen. What happens is that teachers just don't go to a workshop and get trained. They actually see what is going to work with a student right in front of them. They have just learned a skill that way that they didn't have before.

So it is very much a process where the team is important in supporting teachers, but the other part of the process is this in-class searching for what works in a very trial and error way. Again, from where we were 10 years ago, we have got much better ideas about what to use. Frankly, at this point, a combination of a strong foundational early literacy program with a process that helps teachers with kids that are falling even out of that good program would be a very strong complementary program.

Mr. Wilson. And during the IST period, the 50-day period of determination, are parents notified or are they involved?

Mr. Kovaleski. They are actively involved. It is interesting that we didn't even start with that as a training component in 1990. The schools did that themselves. They got parents to the table early and talked over what was going on. We had extremely harmonious and effective relationships with parents. We did parent training in that process. Interestingly, parents were more than happy to come to school if you get them early in the process rather than waiting for their reaction later.

Mr. Wilson. And that is through parents being involved?

Mr. Kovaleski. Absolutely.

Mr. Wilson. And so much being put on the teachers, that concern me.

And for Mr. Gordon, I want to congratulate you. You had indicated no litigation. That is extraordinary.

Mr. Gordon. Thank you, sir.

Mr. Wilson. You must be working with parents, and so that is a great sign.

Mr. Gordon. Yes, the thing that we do that I think is effective, which could be applied to the whole IDEA. The first time the parent encounters the system, so to speak, is at the IEP meeting. We work hard to train people to facilitate the IEP meetings. We used in our collective bargaining process, a process called interest-based bargaining. So they are trained to facilitate the meetings so the parents first encounter with the system is positive. And we work to seek solutions in terms of the program that is planned for the student.

Mr. Wilson. Well, I certainly hope other people can learn from your example and that can spread.

Additionally, I was interested in your point about over-enrollment. I heard you indicate that there was a waiver that had to be sought. Was that due to federal regulation, state regulation, or what was the regulation that needed to be waived?

Mr. Gordon. Both. At the time, you couldn't use special education money unless the child had an IEP. So actually it was a two-sided waiver. We got the waiver to use the special ed personnel with children who are not yet identified. But the other thing that was important to us that we got was a hold harmless so that we didn't lose money if this whole thing worked. This allowed us to reinvest the money back into the early intervention system. Since the state law has been changed basically to make it a capitated program, you get funded for a certain proportion of your kids and then you keep the difference if you don't identify that many. So there is no more need for waivers.

Mr. Wilson. So much now goes back to the local school district to make that determination, is that correct?

Mr. Gordon. Right, right. But the fact of the matter is in the long run we haven't saved money because we are serving many, many more low incident students with very costly services.

Mr. Wilson. Intensive. Thank you, Mr. Chairman.

Chairman Castle. Thank you, Mr. Wilson.

Ms. Davis?

Mrs. Davis. Thank you, Mr. Chairman. And I also wanted to thank the expert panelists and particularly an old and dear friend, Mr. Gordon, who I want to just share with you that the Elk

Grove School District is really among the best in the state of California and certainly the nation. And Mr. Gordon has brought that to the district, and I want to applaud him for that.

Mr. Gordon. Thank you.

Mrs. Davis. I think you really have just touched on the issue that I was particularly concerned about, and that is teacher preparation and training and in collaboration with parents. Is there anything in the reauthorization now that we are looking at that needs to be enhanced to really support that issue? In San Diego, I must admit, they actually tried to have teachers in regular classrooms with some special education expertise, and frankly, it didn't work. And the district came under great fire as a result of it from parents as well as from the state of California. And so they certainly have to go back and take a look at the way that was occurring in the school district.

I am just looking now as we actually are working with language, it sounds like you have what you need there to do what is possible. But I want to be sure that school districts perhaps that are not aware of the need, it is the collaboration. It is the feedback for teachers. It is not just the hour on a Saturday, it is having somebody in the classroom who is really letting them know that this is working or not working or they are able to evaluate it certainly on their own. And in a lot of school districts, we don't necessarily have that peer support. We don't provide it. We don't fund it. We don't do a whole lot of things to encourage it. And sometimes there is a lot of resistance as well.

Is there anything that we particularly should be looking at that would aid you in that and obviously would help kids, which is what we are all about here?

Mr. Kovaleski. I am going to have a really hard time giving you advice about how to change the law or if the law needs to be changed about that. However, I can clearly articulate what the problem is, and maybe that will help us get part of the way. We are going through a real sea change in education. I think for the first time in my 25 years, we have actually seen people start to say, ``Let's look at what works for kids from a scientific research point of view." Throughout all my years, the thing that has frustrated me the most about being in education is that it is who has got the new idea before it has even been tested. If we had anything in public education that I would love to have it is an FDA for instructional strategies. Let's make sure that we are using what has been proven to work, not what somebody came up with last week and is already selling their product to schools.

I think we need to look at getting everybody focused on outcomes, holding people's feet to the fire as to whether those are not working, and using research-based approaches. If things are not working, let's look at what we need to do to change from systems that are using ineffective instructional strategies to those that are. How you change college education systems to have people teach new teachers strategies that work and not the 49 ideas about what might work is very daunting to me but that is what needs to happen.

Mrs. Davis. Thank you. Anybody else want to respond?

Mr. Lyon. Well, actually, David should go before me, because he has done an extremely creative thing in Elk Grove with teacher preparation, which maybe he will share. But I would just like to reinforce Dr. Kovaleski's point in terms of changing the emphasis to what works and how it affects kids.

For the last 30 years, everything seems to have been done for the adult's sake. We still have to deal with funding research that adults do because the adults want to do the research irrespective of whether it helps kids. Likewise, we continue to put programs in schools that people like, but don't work. The reason they continue to stay there is based upon belief and philosophy. I think Joe is absolutely correct. Once we start to operate from the very clear window of what works, we need to examine the evidence.

I think in the situation or the example that I gave in Florida and in David's example in California, people rally around what works. In the 39,000 kids we have studied and the over 1,200 schools we have studied, it is very difficult to change teachers' minds by quacking away at them. What changes their minds is watching kids actually change. Kids don't get better and don't develop better skills, unless somebody is using what has been shown to work.

The chairman earlier asked about Reading First and Early Reading First and how all of this integrates with that. Secretary Pasternack is working extremely hard on commensurate language to say that we should not be spending federal money on programs, projects, strategies or approaches that haven't been shown to be effective with the kids that you have in your district. We have got to support schools better that way. I think that as culture shifts from process to what works and from philosophy and belief to science, then people start to get on the same page with a common language. I think it is going to take that. In the law, we have a very clear statement that we should not be spending taxpayer money for that which is shown to be ineffective. In our experience, that is what will drive the common language, the collaboration, and the communication.

Mr. Gordon. Just one other comment. I think in your law you can push the higher education people much harder to collaborate with school districts. We got frustrated about eight or nine years ago so we run our own teacher credential program, because we were getting people coming out who were mis-trained. We had to retrain them and we changed the whole program. So now we have doubled the amount of time they spend hands-on in the classroom. And we added two extra courses in reading so they are trained then to our specifications. We are about to start up a comparable program for special education.

Chairman Castle. Thank you, Ms. Davis.

Mrs. Davis. Thank you, Mr. Chairman.

Chairman Castle. I haven't asked questions yet, but I am going to go to Mr. Payne first. Then unless anybody else comes, I will go last and we will finish it up there.

Mr. Payne?

Mr. Payne. Thank you very much. It is kind of unusual for a chairman to be so benevolent, but I certainly appreciate that.

I just have a question. As a former educator, many years ago, I certainly have had some concerns throughout the years, even when I was teaching, about the over-representation of minorities. Data suggest that racial and ethnic distribution of students in special ed essentially remains unchanged from 1998 to 1999 school year. Black students, however, continue to be over-represented in special education across all disability categories. We go on to find out that all blacks with disabilities is 20.3 percent, which exceeds their representation in the resident population, which is about 14.5 percent.

The most striking disparities were in mental retardation. Over one-third of African-American students were considered mentally retarded, and developmentally delayed was 30.5 percent, and probably leaving only about a third of the population to be in neither category unless there is overlapping. As you mentioned, there are seven categories, and perhaps some of the 30.5 percent might be counted in the other 34.2 percent.

But the other very glowing statistic is that most of these, of course, are boys, are men, young men. So I just have a question. I am not trying to find solutions and I am not being critical, I am just trying to determine whether there is a problem in teacher training, whether cultural - sometimes Hispanics, for example, are supposed to be more Latin and very expressive. Perhaps Haitian Americans because of their culture also tend to be more colorful. We find this problem in law enforcement with someone who might be considered belligerent by say a Caucasian police officer, an African-American who grew up in the same neighborhood, well, that is relatively typical. As a matter of fact, under these circumstances and under the stress that most African-American males have to go through, anyway, they tell me if you don't have high blood pressure and you are a black guy, you haven't done anything.

So you have got these cultural problems that are very difficult. Even in medicine, you find that there is the same kind of disparity even with people who have the same income and same insurance coverage, sometimes not even about access, but it is about the ability to communicate. And we find that there are more health disparities in people who have the same kind of coverage.

So it is kind of what I would like to see if we could determine how we can crack this continuing problem that has been around for a long time and it is not even going to go away even if we start to come up with solutions. So if any of you would take that?

Mr. Lyon. Let me try to unpack the two, the educational from the medical, and go with you on the educational issues. I say very clearly to you, Representative Payne, it does not and should not be that way. The over-representation is a function of the system not providing what is needed with what works. This relates to something that Chairman Castle brought up. Let me first say that the issue that you are talking about on the educational side is neither racial nor ethnic, it is economic. Socioeconomic factors cut through all these kinds of things. No doubt there are cultural issues that you know much more about than I do.

Here is the fact of the matter. In the school that I showed you, the Hartsfield School, the majority of youngsters in this school come from poverty. Sixty percent are on free and reduced lunch. What does that mean? It means frequently that their parents do not read. Because their parents do not read, they are not read to as much as middle class kids and beyond. They are not interacting in discussions and conversations, building vocabulary that other kids with advantage have. They come into preschool and kindergarten way, way behind.

Now, Chairman Goodling remembered the fact that an affluent three-year-old has a stronger working vocabulary than the welfare parent of a three-year-old. That is true. By 18 months of age, kids in middle to affluent families are learning nine new words a day, every day until they move into school. Kids from poverty are learning three to four words, putting a 50 percent differential on language.

Here they come into school. Yes, African-Americans are being over-represented, not because of their race but because poverty is disproportionately represented in those ethnic groups, those and Hispanic kids. As you know, if you just unpack reading, 38 percent of our nation's fourth graders cannot read a lick. If you disaggregate those data, 65 percent of African-American kids can't read very well. And 60 percent of Hispanic kids cannot read.

That is not the effect of a learning disability. That is the effect of accumulating distance from what they should know. They don't have the foundational skills. They come into preschool, kindergarten, first grade, and no one is building the foundation for them. That is why Early Reading First tries to go directly to getting these kids, as Chairman Castle said, not at 5, not at 6, but at 3 and 4 and 5.

We are working very hard on Head Start now to make sure we are infusing in Head Start not only interactions to develop emotional and social capabilities, but language and early literacy capabilities. The system has to step up to the plate. Otherwise, we are going to continue recursively to see this cycle continue. If we don't help kids learn to read, think, write, and to do math, then they are going to have kids that are equally behind the bar.

But that is the real issue. Poverty is cutting no slack in how these kids are learning. By the way, the IQ tests that are given that put these kids disproportionately into mental retardation categories are based not so much on the kid's intelligence but what the kids have learned. An IQ test is nothing more than accumulated knowledge. If you are not being interacted with or your folks are working too hard and have three jobs or if your parents can't read and can't engage you in these interactions, at 2 and 3 and 4 and 5, you are going to be lagging so far behind by the time somebody gives you an IQ test. It is not measuring your intelligence, but is measuring the lack of interaction.

Guess what is going to be the solution? Early identification, early intervention from birth onward and strong, and strong teaching and instruction that is based upon the scientific evidence. When we do that, those kids you are talking about now are no longer put behind by what the President calls that ``soft bigotry of low expectation." We now have 3.7 kids in first grades having difficulties learning to read in a highly disadvantaged school, whereas when we started 31.8 percent were learning. That is because the system responded to those needs.

Mr. Kovaleski. If I can add to that just briefly. Since the '70s we were asking for culture-fair testing, we still don't have it. There are no tests that are going to be fair to all the cultures that we have in schools. We talked earlier about response to instructions being the way to identify whether students need special education. I think this is the way to be fair to everybody, especially minority students, because we can see their rate of learning when we carefully teach them. The problem with that is going to be that when kids come to school so far behind, as Dr. Lyon is talking about, it is nice to see the Hartsfield data but in many cases they are not going to catch up overnight.

I cannot tell you how many times in my career I have heard people say, ``I know this kid doesn't have a learning disability, but the only way to get him help is to put him in special education." That is not fair to anybody. We have got to look at ways that we can improve general education so that during the primary years, especially, we can provide the intensity of programs that are as intense as special education without having to label kids and identify them as special ed.

Mr. Payne. Thank you very much. I see my time has expired.

Chairman Castle. Thank you.

Mr. Payne. I would like to go on, but I won't. And maybe, Mr. Chairman, we could work on that jointly some time in the future to take a look at how we can -

Chairman Castle. In fact, I am delighted you raised the question, because I have been bothered by some of those statistics, too. I thought the answers were extremely interesting and extremely thorough. I would be happy to work on it. We have been working on it and the bottom line is that we have just got to do more. I agree that the socioeconomic issue is what it really comes down to that we have to deal with.

Let me just yield to myself for a couple of minutes here in terms of finishing up. Let me start with you, Dr. Lyon. Perhaps I am not as knowledgeable about these programs as I should be. I have always focused more on the B aspect of all this, and the C and D are starting to interest me a little bit. I don't know enough about them to really argue whether the way they were done in the reformation of the law five years ago is the correct way to go or not or if there is inadequate funding in terms of the research and the preparation in the under-three program. But should we be looking more at those programs than perhaps we are focused on? I think most of the time we hear about the B program and not those as much.

Mr. Lyon. Absolutely, Mr. Chairman. I think it is nice to have a question where we have proactively moved forward to bolster both in OSERS and at NIH our efforts from birth to three and birth to five. Beginning in 2003, for the first time we will be working strongly with other agencies, not just in conversation but also in actual planning and in actual investment. Working with Dr. Pasternack's office, OSERS and with HHS to bring together and put in place the largest, most comprehensive research program. This will address how we can get all kids from birth to school entry squared away and learning well in terms of their cognitive language pre-literacy skills integrated with good social competencies and good strong emotional health. For years, people have attacked these issues, if they have attacked them at all, from birth to five in very parochial ways. They have talked about social and emotional development or they have talked about cognitive development. Frankly, they have never been integrated.

Now across agencies we are going to bring to bear our best talent and quite a bit of resources financially to figure out what it is kids need to know, how we can identify if they have it at the earliest ages, if they don't have it, how at the earliest stages we can bolster their development and how to make sure that we are tracking them or following them or walking with them through their life. This allows us to see the effects of our efforts at every epic in their development.

So I will assure you that in 2003 you will see a very well integrated research program across OSERS, across NICHD, and across HHS, ACF and ACYF, that goes directly to what you are talking about.

Chairman Castle. That is comforting, although sometimes I worry about the acronyms and the_

Mr. Lyon. I am sorry.

Chairman Castle. - inability of most of us to be able to relate all those things as to what we are doing.

Mr. Lyon. Right.

Chairman Castle. We are basically trying to help very young kids get a good start is really what it all adds up to.

Mr. Lyon. You got it, yes, sir.

Chairman Castle. I think we need to be clear in our messages as well, but we thank you for your extraordinary work in that area. It is really exceptional.

Let me turn to Dr. Kovaleski and to Mr. Gordon with basically the same question. It is sort of broad and I don't expect you to have a complete knowledge of everything that is in the IDEA law. We write them and we don't have complete knowledge of it. So I know it is a little difficult.

But both of you in your testimony, which I read but did not hear you deliver, unfortunately, indicated that by various practices, which you have adopted in Pennsylvania or in your school district, you have been able to reduce some of the over-identification and deal with some of the statistical problems of IDEA and hopefully this will get kids out of the system earlier and into the regular education system and help educate them more. I assume for the most part that you have done that within the context of the law as it is written today, but I could be wrong about that. Perhaps you have waivers or something, which I don't know about, that have aided you in doing this.

I think, Mr. Gordon, you actually recommended in your testimony some possible changes as far as the federal law is concerned. I am interested to know if a number of the practices that you have employed could be done within the context of the law today. Are there clear recommendations that you have in terms of things we should be looking at to give that flexibility to make sure that we have leaders who can actually make a difference in making IDEA work better and obviously helping kids more?

Mr. Kovaleski. Everything we did in Pennsylvania was within the constructs of IDEA and we had no waivers for any of those programs. They were all understood under the screening aspect of IDEA. In 1997, when you folks gave us the new revised law, one of the most heartening things that we had in there was the response to instruction or the lack of instruction provision. To be identified as eligible for special education, you could not be having your problem because of lack of instruction. That really fits very closely with what we are talking about.

What we need, though, is for people to understand precisely what procedures you go through to assess whether or not there was a lack of instruction involved. That is a key piece of the legislation that currently exists that can be expanded upon in order to deliver the kind of programs that I think we are thinking about.

The other part of it is in the preamble to IDEA. There is wonderful language about pre-referral intervention and teams and so forth, but it doesn't make its way into the statute itself. I think the place where all this belongs is in screening. I think if we can beef up the screening part so that it is clear when we talk about assessing lack of instruction, that we have got to do demonstrated interventions before we even get to testing, regardless of what you want to talk about that conversation. Before we get to testing, let's make sure we have documented interventions based on scientifically researched principles. I think that would really give a clear message to the field.

Chairman Castle. Thank you. Mr. Gordon?

Mr. Gordon. I think the best thing that you can do is change your compliance monitoring oversight system so it provides incentives to do the right thing, screening-wise and instructionally. Right now, no one ever comes and asks you how the program is going instructionally. It is all procedural minutia and piles of paper.

So that is where the accountability comes in. We have got to start asking the right questions about how are we doing instructionally, how are we doing in identification, and have the technical assistance to back that up to get people to where they are talking about changing the culture that Dr. Lyon talked about.

Chairman Castle. Well, let me thank you, Mr. Gordon, for that statement, and Dr. Kovaleski. That brings to an end our questioning. We have a vote, which you may have heard the buzzers starting again. So we will end the entire hearing at this point.

In closing, I would just like - I will turn to Mr. Kildee in a moment- to thank you. I worry sometimes when we are dealing with IDEA, that those who are the advocates for these programs, generally families or those families with children who are in the program or have been in the program or people who are working in the program, become concerned that any change could potentially diminish the law as it is and perhaps be harmful to the ultimate beneficiaries, the children. When in reality I believe that we can make changes and improve the law and provide greater opportunity for these children. I think the testimony from both of our panels today underlines this. I think it is very important that we have that dialogue. There are significant numbers of families in this country who are affected by this.

I am delighted we have the web site now. People can go to it and make further suggestions to us, because we want to have that communication. I don't want to get into a tug of war. I want to get into a meaningful discourse and dialogue to improve this law. We ended up doing that in 1997. I just hope we can do it in 2002. I think this kind of hearing helps with that a lot. So we appreciate the testimony of all of you today.

Mr. Kildee?

Mr. Kildee. Thank you, Mr. Chairman. This has been an excellent hearing. We have heard from a researcher and two great providers who gave us some very, very good insights. Some hearings only rate, C+, some B, but this was a good A+ hearing. Thank you very much.

Chairman Castle. I didn't get a lot of A+'s in school, so I appreciate that.

Thank you all very much. We stand adjourned.

[Whereupon, at 12:50 p.m., the subcommittee was adjourned.]

APPENDIX A - WRITTEN OPENING STATEMENT OF CHAIRMAN MICHAEL CASTLE, SUBCOMMITTEE ON EDUCATION REFORM, COMMITTEE ON EDUCATION AND THE WORKFORCE, U.S. HOUSE OF REPRESENTATIVES, WASHINGTON, D.C.

Statement of the Honorable Michael N. Castle
Chairman, Subcommittee on Education Reform
"Learning Disabilities and Early Intervention Strategies:
How to Improve the Special Education Referral and Identification Process"
June 6, 2002

Good Morning. Welcome to the next in the series of hearings on the reform and reauthorization of the Individuals with Disabilities Education Act, the federal education law which welcomes all learners and excludes none -- regardless of their disability.

Today, children with disabilities sit with their nondisabled peers in regular classrooms, and many learn from a general education curriculum. Yet, despite these significant accomplishments, children with disabilities are not completing school or performing at levels near their nondisabled peers.

As I have stated previously, it is not enough to open the school house door for children with special needs. We must ensure that we meet the letter -- as well as the spirit -- of the law and provide our children with the high quality instruction and services they need to succeed.

Just as we must move states and schools from simple compliance to real achievement, we must also ensure that our special education and general education programs evolve to meet the needs of a new generation of children with disabilities.

Today, more than half of our children in special education programs have specific learning disabilities. Yet, unlike some severe physical and mental disabilities, many children with learning disabilities are identified too late. Others are overidentified because they fail to learn fundamental skills, like reading. In each case, frustration and an accumulated learning gap can spell disaster, with many children dropping out of high school and shunning higher education.

For these reasons, the purpose of this morning's hearing is to learn more about the way students with various learning disabilities are referred for special education and related services under IDEA. Specifically, I want to know how IDEA can be strengthened to prevent mild learning problems from turning into lifelong disabilities.

I also want to know more about the models and strategies that have been effective in helping children learn in new ways.

Finally, I believe it is important to hear more about effective, evidence-based early intervention programs and how they have been used to improve education outcomes. It is my hope that our distinguished witnesses will provide our members a better understanding of each of these issues.

To that end, I am pleased to welcome a mentor and a friend, the former Chairman of the Education and the Workforce Committee, Bill Goodling. Although I was sorry to see him retire to his farm in Seven Valleys, Pennsylvania, his counsel will carry me through IDEA reauthorization -- just as it did with the reauthorization of ESEA. I will proceed with the introduction of the rest of our distinguished panel in just a moment.

First, I want to thank those of you in the audience as well as those listening to our IDEA hearing via live webcast. I know that many of you are interested in communicating directly with the Education and the Workforce Committee on issues related to learning disabilities as well as the other topics in this series.

To that end, my colleagues and I have unveiled a new interactive "Great IDEAs" website on the Education and the Workforce Committee page. This will allow us to hear directly from the teachers and principals, parents and coaches, advocates and relatives who educate and care for our children with disabilities on the upcoming reform.

I know I speak for all committee members when I encourage you to share your thoughts and reauthorization ideas. I look forward to hearing from you all.

Now, let's proceed with the hearing: I yield to the distinguished Ranking Member, Mr. Kildee, for whatever opening statement he may wish to make.

APPENDIX B - WRITTEN OPENING STATEMENT OF RANKING MINORITY MEMBER DALE E. KILDEE, SUBCOMMITTEE ON EDUCATION REFORM, COMMITTEE ON EDUCATION AND THE WORKFORCE, U.S. HOUSE OF REPRESENTATIVES, WASHINGTON, D.C.

Remarks of
The Honorable Dale E. Kildee
Subcommittee Hearing on Learning Disabilities, Identification, and Early Intervention
June 6, 2002

GOOD MORNING, I AM PLEASED TO JOIN GOVERNOR CASTLE AT OUR LATEST HEARING ON REAUTHORIZATION OF IDEA. I WANT TO JOIN GOVERNOR CASTLE IN WELCOMING OUR WITNESSES TO TODAY'S HEARING. I HAD A CHANCE TO MEET WITH ASSISTANT SECRETARY, BOB PASTERNACK BRIEFLY YESTERDAY, AND I AM CERTAIN THE PRAISE HE HAS RECEIVED BY THOSE IN THE FIELD IS INDEED DESERVED. I ALSO WANT TO ESPECIALLY WELCOME MY FRIEND AND FORMER CHAIRMAN OF THIS COMMITTEE BILL GOODLING.

DURING HIS CAREER HERE IN CONGRESS, AND ALSO AS AN EDUCATOR, BILL GOODLING WORKED TIRELESSLY TO PROVIDE FULL FUNDING FOR IDEA, BUT ALSO TO IMPROVE THE LIVES AND EDUCATION OF CHILDREN WITH DISABILITIES. HIS APPEARANCE HERE TODAY SHOWS HIS COMMITMENT TO OUR NATION'S CHILDREN CONTINUES. YOUR LEADERSHIP IN THE CONGRESS ON THESE ISSUES IS MISSED.

TODAY'S FOCUS ON LEARNING DISABILITIES, THEIR IDENTIFICATION, AND THE NEED FOR PRE-REFERRAL BEHAVIOR AND ACADEMIC INTERVENTION SERVICES IS A CRUCIAL ELEMENT OF OUR REVIEW OF IDEA.

ACCORDING TO THE DEPARTMENT'S 23RD ANNUAL REPORT TO CONGRESS, SLIGHTLY LESS THAN HALF OF ALL CHILDREN WITH DISABILITIES ARE IDENTIFIED AS HAVING LEARNING DISABILITIES. WE MUST EXAMINE WHAT SERVICES THESE CHILDREN ARE BEING PROVIDED WITHIN IDEA AND WHAT INTERVENTIONS AND SUPPORTS CAN BE PROVIDED PRIOR TO IDENTIFICATION. THESE INTERVENTIONS AND SUPPORTS CAN MAKE SPECIAL EDUCATION UNNECESSARY FOR A NUMBER OF

CHILDREN. HOWEVER, SOME WITH IDENTIFIED LEARNING DISABILITIES WILL ALWAYS NEED THE PROTECTIONS AND SERVICES PROVIDED UNDER IDEA.

IN ANY DISCUSSION OF INTERVENTION SERVICES DESIGNED TO REDUCE MISIDENTIFICATION, WE MUST ENSURE THAT THESE SERVICES DO NOT CREATE BARRIERS TO THOSE WHO NEED SPECIAL EDUCATION.

EQUALLY IMPORTANT IN OUR DISCUSSION OF INTERVENTION SERVICES IS THE NEED TO HAVE THEM ADDRESS BOTH ACADEMIC AND BEHAVIORAL DIFFICULTIES. A GREAT DEAL OF ATTENTION HAS FOCUSED ON CHILDREN WHO STRUGGLE IN READING. INTERVENTION STRATEGIES MUST ALSO ADDRESS FUNCTIONAL AND BEHAVIORAL PROBLEMS THAT CHILDREN EXPERIENCE.

LASTLY, OUR EFFORTS TO EXAMINE THE IDENTIFICATION PROCESS AND ITS IMPACT ON CHILDREN MUST BE DONE CAREFULLY. WE NEED TO CONTINUE TO FOCUS OUR EFFORTS ON FULL IMPLEMENTATION OF IDEA, RATHER THAN SEEKING CHANGES IN STATUTE MERELY FOR THE SAKE OF CHANGE. THIS TRANSLATES INTO BETTER TECHNICAL ASSISTANCE FROM THE DEPARTMENT TO STATES AND FROM THE STATES TO SCHOOL DISTRICTS. IN ADDITION, IT ALSO DEMANDS A STRONGER ENFORCEMENT ROLE BY THE DEPARTMENT AND POSSIBLY OTHER AGENCIES TO TARGET SERIOUS ISSUES OF NONCOMPLIANCE WITH THE STATUE.

IN CLOSING MR. CHAIRMAN, I WANT TO THANK YOU FOR HOLDING THIS HEARING AND LOOK FORWARD TO WORKING WITH YOU ON REAUTHORIZATION IN THE COMING MONTHS AND NEXT YEAR.

THANK YOU MR. CHAIRMAN.

APPENDIX C - WRITTEN STATEMENT OF HON. WILLIAM F. GOODLING, FORMER CHAIRMAN, COMMITTEE ON EDUCATION AND THE WORKFORCE, WASHINGTON, D.C.

TESTIMONY OF THE HONORABLE WILLIAM F. GOODLING, FORMER CHAIRMAN, COMMITTEE ON EDUCATION AND THE WORKFORCE

Before the Subcommittee on Education Reform

"Learning Disabilities and Early Intervention Strategies: How to Reform the Special Education Referral and Identification Process"

Thursday, June 6, 2002 10:00 a.m.
2175 Rayburn House Office Building

Thank you Chairman Castle and Members of the Subcommittee for this opportunity to share my views on the upcoming renewal of IDEA. This is my first time back testifying before the Committee. I'm glad to see that, even though I'm not here on a daily basis as before, I still am looking over your shoulder as you consider the important issues concerning the education of children in America.

In my judgement there is no more pressing issue facing this Committee right now than what brings us together this morning. As the chief author of the last reauthorization of the Individuals with Disabilities Education Act (IDEA), I am pleased that you Mr. Chairman, Chairman Boehner, Congressman Kildee and Ranking Member Miller are moving forward with rewriting this landmark Act. It is my hope that Congress will continue to improve on the reforms that we put into place five years ago.

In its 27 year life span, IDEA has achieved many goals in serving children with disabilities and guaranteeing rights and opportunities for each child. The debate today is no longer about whether children with disabilities will have access to a free and appropriate public education. Those battles have been fought and won. This success, however, has not come about without problems.

Chairman Castle was astute as always when he declared at an earlier hearing this year: "I believe (we) must build on the positive changes made in the 1997 reauthorization and allow this law to evolve. No longer is it simply enough to provide our disabled children access to public schools."

When I was appointed Chairman of this Committee in 1994, I immediately began to address the problems with our system of educating children with unique challenges.

At that time, as today, federal funding of IDEA was of major and growing concern. We were the first to call on Congress to uphold the government's promise to pay for 40 percent of the national average expenditure for non-disabled students to assist states and local educational agencies with the excess costs of educating children with disabilities.

Eight years ago that seemed like an unlikely outcome. But, as you know, since then Congress has made great strides in working toward that goal. Through both the authorizing and appropriations process we added over a billion dollars each year toward the goal.

In fact, during my last year in Congress, I introduced legislation with Chairman Castle's, Ranking Member Kildee's, and many other Members' support to ensure that this 40% federal funding goal would be met by the fiscal year 2010. The House passed that bill by a vote of 421-3, however the Senate did not follow suit.

Accomplishments of the Individuals with Disabilities Education Act Amendments of 1997

I think it might be helpful to the more junior Members of the Committee to recall a few of the steps we accomplished in our rewriting of the Act five years ago.

In 1996, the House passed the IDEA Improvement Act by a unanimous vote. Our goal was to increase the educational opportunities available to children with disabilities. We plowed new ground by:

- **Focusing on academic achievement and placing an emphasis on what is best educationally;**
- **Giving teachers more flexibility and schools lower costs;**
- **Enhancing parental input;**
- **Making schools safer for students and teachers; and**
- **Consolidating special education discretionary programs.**

Once again, despite our efforts, the Senate did not act on our legislation.

Finally, thanks to the Members of this Committee and others in Congress who supported the effort, in 1997 Congress passed historic legislation to reform IDEA. During my years in Congress, I knew of no other major authorizing legislation that had gone through the same consensus process, with all major stakeholders in the room including the Administration, to produce a bipartisan, bicameral bill.

These monumental reforms focused on children's education instead of process and bureaucracy, giving parents greater input in determining the best education for their child, and giving teachers the tools they need to teach all children well.

Funding and Accountability

I'm hearing from all sides in this debate that the changes we made in 1997 are just now beginning to generate improvements. In the lifetime of a law, IDEA is just beginning the implementation phase. In fact, this regulation-burdened law didn't have new rules finalized until almost two years after its enactment. This is important for Members of this Committee and others in Congress to remember as new reforms are considered.

With the new discussion on issues to consider in the law's renewal, much of the debate has centered on problems we addressed in the last reauthorization. Airing of continuing difficulties are an important part of the oversight and legislative process. And while the last set of changes are taking affect, I agree that some additional reforms are in order.

For instance, any legislation this year should reinforce student results and academic achievement, and expand on the state accountability standards that were put into place since 1997.

However, creating additional federal mandates in a law that is already overloaded with regulations and requirements could result in exacerbating problems that have slowed the educational progress of children with disabilities.

As I noted, Congress has nearly tripled funding the IDEA over the past six years, and this trend is likely to continue. Congress must develop a consistent appropriations process to deliver on its promise to states and school districts who face rising costs of educating the over 6.5 million children who are now receiving special educational services.

This year, with the president's leadership, we are looking at the possibility of more than $1 billion in additional federal support in special education. This is a rational and consistent effort to meet our commitments.

Preparing Teachers

Teaching children with disabilities can be both the most rewarding and the most arduous job in teaching. We need professionals who not only have the commitment, but the skills in the classroom and with parents, to help students succeed. A tall order by any estimation.

As I often said while I was Chairman, a child's first and most important teachers are his or her parents. And waiting for that child at the schoolhouse door need to be teachers who understand the complexities of early instruction.

The educational progress of children with disabilities depends on proper teacher training for both special education and regular classroom teachers. Most general classroom teachers receive little or no pre-service training for instructing children with disabilities. Many have just a few classes on disabilities in college. While at the same time, new regular teachers start their classroom instruction with, on average, four IDEA students in their classes.

The President's "Leave No Child Behind" law contains important progress in the area of recruitment and training for elementary school teachers. Similar to these provisions in Title II of ESEA, Congress should strengthen the role of partnerships between institutions of higher education and school districts in training IDEA practitioners.

The special education field has been hit hard by the critical teacher shortage facing our nation. We must find ways to encourage students to enter the profession, especially in rural and urban areas. In the House we made progress in this regard under the old Title VI with specific language in the FY 2000 and 2001 appropriations bills. I hope you will consider additional incentives in this regard.

Today's system is set up not so much to reward teachers and schools that demonstrate behavioral and academic achievement for students with disabilities, but to penalize those who don't respond as the regulations envision.

While we cannot weaken requirements that guarantee a free and appropriate public education for all students, it makes perfect sense to strengthen financial incentive grants to those who demonstrate a commitment to work with each child and their family to reach their full education potential, to graduation, job training, and beyond.

Stronger Emphasis on Mediation to Reduce Litigation

The judicial processes in special education litigation are too costly and distracting to the point that oftentimes a child's education is lost in the back and forth. In some cases, the judgement of trained teachers is ignored because school districts, understandably, opt to settle a case to avoid the high costs of due process.

Congress should place a stronger emphasis on mediation to reduce litigation so that parents and schools are encouraged to resolve their differences with a child's best interests in mind, and that is consistent with the appropriate education of the child.

It is my strong belief that in cases where due process is pursued, attorney's fees must continue to be limited to discourage those who seek to take advantage of the system.

Relief of the Paperwork Burden

A nearly universal complaint from all parties in special education is the burden of paperwork. Teachers, parents, and other Individual Education Plan (IEP) participants, feel overwhelmed by the amount of forms they have to track. In particular, the time spent by teachers filling out paperwork deprives them of the time that should be spent with planning and interacting with students.

Congress should explore ways to combine funds from a variety of sources to help schools and districts better use technology to reduce the paperwork load. More accurate methodologies using modern technology could greatly reduce the amount of time spent filling out forms. Providing that IDEA technology costs are allowable expenses under more federal programs, including E-Rate, and encouraging partnerships with private industries to fund the costs could accelerate technological advances in this regard. In addition, duplicative or unnecessary forms should be eliminated. States and local school districts should be given incentives to encourage the review of existing requirements they perceive necessary to meet federal law.

Early Intervention through Reading and Family Literacy

It is my firm belief that IDEA reforms must strengthen the early identification and diagnosis of any learning, physical and emotional problems in children. Research has confirmed that the earlier children are identified and receive services, the better the chance they have to succeed in regular classrooms.

Over the years as we have attempted to legislate from Washington protections for children with disabilities, the system has responded by corralling children with a wide variety of skills. Neither the action nor reaction has produced desirable results. Students in IDEA programs run the gamut from mild reading difficulties to severe disabilities. Too often they are assigned to the same special education processes. The earlier and more precise our diagnostic efforts are, the better equipped we'll be to provide children the individual and consistent attention their needs may require. The law should reflect this.

In this effort, early childhood reading and research-based family literacy programs must be strengthened to prevent the over-identification of children into special education and reduce the amount of children who are commonly misdiagnosed.

In order to succeed in school, children need the support of their parents. Many parents do not have the literacy and other skills necessary to support their child's education. Additionally, all federally-sponsored pre-school programs should employ research-based literacy programs so that any potential literacy problems, whether it is the child or the parent, are addressed early. Therefore, targeting money to strengthen research-based early reading and family literacy problems would help to prevent inappropriate referrals.

With the President's leadership, Congress took an important step in this direction with the enactment of the Early Reading First initiative. Now those three to six year olds from low-income families who enter Head Start, Even Start, or other community-based early learning programs, will get the evaluation and cognitive development focus necessary to determine the best education-based program to meet their needs. This model needs to be replicated beyond the limited scope of Early Reading First and incorporated into IDEA reforms.

It is also important to increase funding for the programs under Part D, which play an essential role in the development and evaluation of effective practices. This funding has supported practical research into the best methods for identifying and educating children with developmental disabilities.

More research is needed, as is the case with the rapidly increasing number of children diagnosed with autism, to better identify promising practices that ensure early interventions are employed. The sooner children receive help, the earlier they will become as independent as possible. Unfortunately, the funding available for these activities has not kept pace with the need for advanced research.

Later some will need the assistance provided through the IDEA, but some will hopefully get the early instruction that moves them right into general education classes upon entering school. This model needs to be replicated beyond the limited scope of Early Reading First.

The costs expended for the early recognition of problems will pay dividends ten-fold in saved IDEA costs.

Parental Involvement

Federal education initiatives must seek ways to foster, not diminish, parental involvement and responsibility. We must encourage parental involvement without dictating how to remain involved in their child's education.

In the 1997 rewrite, we established a procedure of benchmarks in the IEP process for use by parents, students and instructors. The law provides guidance for setting goals and scheduled reviews. This concept is underutilized and not successfully administered in many IEPs. A renewed emphasis in the process could provide early warnings and help all parties to remain focused on the child's progress, mark milestones, and aid in the development of a healthy dialogue among IEP participants.

Finally, let me say how encouraged I am that this subcommittee is forging ahead with this reauthorization. Your task is great, but so will be the rewards of obtaining a consensus. My only advice is to move forward expeditiously, the costs of delay in both fiscal and human terms are too great to be deterred or delayed.

Again, thank you Chairman Castle and Members of the Subcommittee for this opportunity. I look forward to answering your questions.

APPENDIX D - WRITTEN STATEMENT OF ROBERT PASTERNACK, ASSISTANT SECRETARY FOR SPECIAL EDUCATION AND REHABILITATION SERVICES, U.S. DEPARTMENT OF EDUCATION, WASHINGTON, D.C.

DEPARTMENT OF EDUCATION

Statement by

Robert Pasternack
Assistant Secretary for
Special Education and Rehabilitative Services

On

Learning Disabilities

Before the U.S. House of Representatives
Education and the Workforce
Subcommittee on Education Reform

Mr. Chairman, members of the committee, I want to thank you for the opportunity to appear before you today to discuss issues relating to learning disabilities. As you are no doubt aware, the Individuals with Disabilities Education Act (IDEA) defines a learning disability as a "disorder in one or more of the basic psychological processes involved in understanding or in using spoken or written language, which may manifest itself in an imperfect ability to listen, think, speak, read, write, spell, or to do mathematical calculations." Learning disability is not a single disorder and the various types of disabilities frequently co-occur with one another and with social skill deficits and emotional behavioral disorders. In addition, these problems may mildly, moderately, or severely impair the learning process. We know that children identified as having specific learning disabilities may have problems that affect many areas of learning. However, I want to focus my remarks today on the area of reading. The development of reading skills serves as the major foundational academic ability for all school-based learning.

Our research at the Office of Special Education and Rehabilitative Services (OSERS) and the Office of Educational Research and Improvement (OERI) and the research at the National Institute of Child Health and Development (NICHD), has consistently shown that if children do not learn to understand and use language, to read and write, to calculate and reason mathematically, to solve problems, and to communicate their ideas and perspectives, their opportunities for a fulfilling and rewarding life are seriously compromised.

Specifically, we have learned that school failure has devastating consequences with respect to self-esteem, social development, and opportunities for advanced education and meaningful employment. Nowhere are these consequences of academic failure more apparent than when children fail to learn to read. The development of reading skills serves as the major foundational academic ability for all school-based learning. Without the ability to read, the opportunities for academic and occupational success are limited.

The President and the Congress have clearly recognized the pivotal importance of reading in the No Child Left Behind (NCLB) Act, and in particular the Reading First and Early Reading First initiatives supported through NCLB. The NCLB requires that States and school districts focus on reading through the development of scientifically-based programs, strategies, and materials that will help ensure that all children learn to read. And just as importantly, the law holds States and school districts accountable for achieving results. This strong emphasis on reading is intended to get schools to use scientifically-based reading instruction that incorporates what we know about what works in the teaching of reading – things like phonemic awareness, phonics, fluency, vocabulary, and reading comprehension.

Scope of the Problem

It is clear from research conducted by OSERS and the NICHD that reading failure affects children earlier and more intensely than we previously thought. By the end of the first grade, children displaying difficulty learning to read begin to feel less positive about themselves than when they started school. In later years, these children experience even further decline in self-esteem and motivation. The consequences are dire.

According to the National Center for Education Statistics (NCES, 2000), thirty-seven percent of fourth graders nationally cannot read at a basic level. They cannot read and understand a short paragraph of the type one would find in a simple children's book. For children living in poverty, these statistics are even worse. In many low-income urban school districts the percentage of students in the fourth grade who cannot read at a basic level approaches seventy percent. Nearly half of the 6.5 million children with disabilities receiving special education are identified as having a specific learning disability. Of the 2.8 million children with a specific learning disability, approximately 80 percent to 90 percent have their primary difficulties in learning to read. Of the children who will eventually drop out of school, over seventy-five percent will report difficulties in learning to read. Surveys of adolescents and young adults with criminal records indicate that many have reading difficulties. Approximately half of children and adolescents with a history of substance abuse have reading problems. Needless to say, the inability of many of our nation's children to develop basic reading skills is not just an education problem, it is national social and health problem as well.

Reading Problems and Special Education

While reading is important for all children, it is especially important for children with disabilities. Most of the available information and research on learning disabilities is in the area of reading difficulties. This information has been extremely valuable in our understanding of reading difficulties.

Recent OSERS and NICHD-funded research indicates that many children with deficits in the area of reading can learn to read at "nearly normal" levels when scientifically-based reading instruction is used. However, we also know that some children with reading related learning disabilities do not significantly improve their reading skills even when provided scientifically-based classroom instruction by highly qualified and highly trained personnel. We do not fully understand what conditions need to be in place to remediate the severe intractable reading difficulties of these children.

However, we do know that these children will require specially designed instruction delivered through the IDEA.

Providing the appropriate supports to children who learn to read with varying degrees of ease requires understanding the range of reading difficulties and the concomitant range of interventions needed to serve all children. Primary prevention involves universal assessment and instruction, such as research based schoolwide reading programs, to avert the onset of reading deficits and identify those at risk of failing to learn to read and providing early intervention to those that need it. Secondary prevention refers to scientifically-based strategies and procedures that quickly improve reading skills while they are still emerging. For example, services provided through Title I of the ESEA and other compensatory or supplemental education programs are secondary interventions. Both primary and secondary interventions can include working with small groups of students who need additional support or assistance to successfully acquire skills in reading. The final level of intervention, the tertiary level, involves providing more intense, scientifically-based specialized instruction, such as one-on-one interventions for individual students.

Additional research is needed, however, to identify interventions that will be effective in helping those children with intractable reading problems. Without such research, approximately six percent of all children, those with the most severe reading difficulties, may never gain the skills or opportunity necessary to achieve proficiency. This research must also help us differentiate those children with reading problems who are instructional casualties, children who could learn to read if provided with the appropriate scientifically-based instruction, from those with actual specific learning disabilities. The remaining children, those who do not respond to the scientifically-based interventions we have identified so far, are the right children to bring into special education. One significant challenge is to ensure that we help schools make these differentiations and to conduct research that will identify the right interventions to use with the right children to achieve the right result.

What we must do

In order to improve results for children with learning disabilities, we must be willing to challenge the past and build on what we know. We must take the necessary steps to increase our knowledge base and implement scientifically-based best practices.

First, we must build on the principles embodied in the NCLB Act. Specifically, we must focus on accountability for achieving results for all children including children with disabilities. Also in line with the principles of NCLB, we must focus our efforts on disseminating what works. We must identify and share best practices and not be afraid to discard those that do not yield the results that our children deserve.

Second, we will never help children with disabilities, especially those with learning disabilities, by focusing only on those who are in special education. It is important to understand that many children, including many who are not in special education, have difficulty in learning to read. This is clearly an area where what benefits children with disabilities will benefit all children who have difficulty learning how to read.

Third, we must be adamant about our goal to use scientifically-based instruction and ensure that it is provided only by highly trained and qualified teachers and other paraprofessionals. As you will hear from others asked to testify here today, so much more is being learned from the scientific community than we have ever known about the nature of reading and language acquisition. We need to continue to draw on that knowledge, and promote the development of new knowledge through careful targeting of research resources, partnering with other organizations like NICHD, and, finally, disseminating what we learn.

Fourth, now that we have the tools to help many children who have difficulty in reading, both those who are identified as learning disabled and those who are not, we must increase our efforts to help those children who are considered to have intractable reading difficulties. These are the children who without question need the benefits of IDEA-supported programs.

Fifth, as we think about the use of existing research and the need for future research, we must stress the importance of collaboration in research and in practice. Like research in so many other fields, those of us who are concerned about serving children with disabilities must reach out to the scientific community, the medical community, and others whose work can inform and improve ours. We need to continue to leverage our resources to partner with entities such as NICHD and others. While we have done that in the past and are doing so now, I believe that we must increase our collaborative efforts in research and best practices.

Finally, we must specifically focus attention on methods and strategies for prevention, early identification and early intervention. We need to identify and serve children sooner who need reading and other learning interventions. We know that effective early interventions work. The more children that we can reach early with effective interventions, especially in the area of reading, the more we will be able to help and, in some cases, reduce or even eliminate the need for future special education services. We must also develop solid prevention models that will keep many children from ever needing reading remediation. Helping children with a range of reading difficulties early will help us to focus intensively on those students who do not respond to early interventions.

I firmly believe that the provision of effective services to the children in special education who have learning disabilities is a high priority. We must indeed do more, not just because children with learning disabilities comprise such a large percentage of all disabled children, but we can do more. The convergence of scientific research about LD, especially reading difficulties associated with LD, has placed us on the edge of new knowledge that we did not have even a few short years ago. We now know, for example, that the way we have traditionally looked at assessment of learning disabilities needs to be re-thought based on recent research in the use and role of IQ tests in assessments for eligibility. We know that using IQ discrepancy between the test and performance is not always an indicator of a learning disability. Indeed, some research indicates that if a child who reads slowly has IQ scores that are above average, that child might receive services under the IDEA based on the discrepancy between the IQ scores and the reading ability. On the other hand, another child who also reads slowly but has IQ scores that are average may not receive any services because of the lack of a significant discrepancy.

Such approaches to assessment may clearly result in some children who need services not getting them while others who do not need them will receive them.

We have much to do in serving the 2.8 million children with learning disabilities. There is clearly a need for continued research and clearly a need for us to better use the research that we already have. We must look for results, not promises in what we do. I look forward to working with you, Mr. Chairman, and other members of this committee as we move forward in improving the lives of all children through the IDEA.

I will be happy to answer any questions you may have.

APPENDIX E - WRITTEN STATEMENT OF G. REID LYON, RESEARCH PSYCHOLOGIST AND CHIEF, CHILD DEVELOPMENT AND BEHAVIOR BRANCH, NATIONAL INSTITUTE OF CHILD HEALTH AND HUMAN DEVELOPMENT, ROCKVILLE, MARYLAND

Testimony of Dr. Reid Lyon
Subcommittee on Education Reform
June 6, 2002

Good Morning, Chairman Castle and members of the Subcommittee. I am Dr. Reid Lyon, Chief of the Child Development and Behavior Branch at the National Institute of Child Health and Human Development (NICHD) at the National Institutes of Health. I am honored to have been asked by the Subcommittee to address issues relevant to learning disabilities (LD) and early intervention strategies and how research bearing on these issues can serve to inform the special education referral and identification process.

The testimony that I will present for the record this morning will build on the compelling testimony presented by Dr. Robert Pasternack, Assistant Secretary for the Office of Special Education and Rehabilitative Services (OSERS) within the U.S. Department of Education. I would like to note that the Department of Health and Human Services and the Department of Education have collaborated to identify and address issues that are critical to the health and education of our nation's children. For the first time, the NICHD and OSERS are working hand in hand to ensure that the best research supported by both agencies is integrated and deployed to answer important questions about how to best educate our youngest citizens. Moreover, under the leadership of Secretary Thompson and Secretary Paige, the NICHD is also working closely with Dr. Wade Horn of the Administration for Children and Families (ACF), Dr. Susan Neuman from the Office of Elementary and Secondary Education and Dr. Russ Whitehurst from the Office of Educational Research and Improvement. This collaboration is designed to develop a coordinated effort to ensure that children from birth to adulthood have access to the most supportive and instructive early childhood environments, preschool, and kindergarten experiences that lead to optimal cognitive, social, emotional, and academic development. Let me now turn to the critical issues to be addressed today.

The Critical Need to Improve Identification and Instructional Practices for Students with LD

The Subcommittee's focus today on how best to identify and provide effective services to students with LD is critical given that it is the most frequently identified class of disabilities among students in public schools. This focus takes on additional importance given that the identification and provision of services to students with LD typically takes place within a context of persistent debate about (a) the definition of the disability, (b) the diagnostic criteria and assessment procedures employed in the identification process, (c) the content, intensity, and duration of instructional practices provided, and (d) the policies and legal requirements that guide the identification and education of students with LD.

Increase in Identification of LD at older Ages Not Accompanied by Increases in Student Learning

Since the 1976-1977 school year, when Congress first required public schools to document the number of children with LD, the share of school-age students identified as LD has risen from 1.8 percent to .2 percent. Learning disabilities now account for more than half of all students enrolled in special education programs, an increase of 22 percentage points over the past 25 years. In the past decade alone, the share of students ages 6 to 21 identified as LD under IDEA has increased to 38 percent. The largest increase, 44 percent, is among adolescents ages 12-17.

Unfortunately, this rise in the identification of students with LD often does not lead to improvements in learning, particularly in older students (nine years of age and above) and particularly in reading skills. For example, Eric Hanushek and his colleagues found that placement in special education was associated with a gain of 0.04 standard deviations in reading and 0.11 standard deviations in mathematics. Unfortunately, these gains are so small that children are still not performing at their full potential. This lack of improvement has the further negative effect of keeping students in special education for lengthy periods of time.

This increase in the identification of LD without concomitant improvement in academic achievement among school-age students invites several timely questions. What explains the increase? Is the increase due to improved identification practices? Or is the definition of LD too general and ambiguous to identify younger children at risk for learning failure before they fail? Are some students identified as LD having difficulties learning primarily because of poor instruction? Put another way, does the education profession create instructional casualties by inadequately preparing both general education and special education teachers to address learning differences among children? Once identified, why are special education services not effective in improving learning? Most importantly, can answers to these questions lead to improvements in how LD is defined, how it is identified, how it is prevented, and how children who appear initially unresponsive to early interventions can be taught effectively with effective remedial strategies?

Explanations for Increases in Identification of LD Derived from Converging Research Findings

I will propose today, on the basis of strong converging scientific evidence, that the increase in the incidence of LD is related to four factors. First, the vague definition of LD currently in Federal law and the use of invalid eligibility criteria (e.g., IQ-achievement discrepancies) invite variability in identification procedures. For instance, LD identification processes, particularly with regard to how test scores are used, differ across states and even across local school districts within states. Thus, the identification of students with LD is a highly subjective process. In some states, and even in some local school districts, different diagnostic criteria are used. For example, one state or local district may require a 22-point discrepancy between an IQ and an achievement test, while another state or district requires more or fewer points, or does not require an IQ-achievement discrepancy calculation at all.

Second, and clearly related to increases in referral for assessment of LD, traditional approaches to reading instruction in the early grades have substantially underestimated the variability among children in their talent and preparation for learning to read. We have seen that many teachers have not been prepared to address and respond to the individual differences in learning that students bring to the classroom. A significant number of general education teachers report that their training programs did not prepare them to properly assess learner characteristics and provide effective reading instruction on the basis of these assessments, particularly to children with limited oral language and literacy experiences who arrive in the classroom behind in vocabulary development, print awareness abilities, and phonological abilities. Our data suggest that many of these youngsters have difficulties reading, not because they are LD, but because they are initially behind and do not receive the classroom instruction that can build the necessary foundational language and early reading skills. If a student is not succeeding academically, general education teachers tend to refer them for specialized services. While some children require these services, many may only require informed classroom instruction from a well-prepared classroom teacher. Well-prepared is the operative term here; when teachers do not receive the benefits of robust training, many children entering their classrooms who require differentiated instruction to address these learning needs leave the classrooms as instructional casualties and/or referrals to special education.

Third, given that remediation of learning difficulties is minimally effective after the second grade, it is especially troubling that there has been a large increase in the identification of learning disabilities of students in the later grades. We have theorized that this is primarily due to students falling further and further behind in their academic progress because of reading difficulties and losing motivation to succeed rather than due to limitations in brain plasticity or the closing of "critical periods" in which learning can occur. Consider, during the time that students have been allowed to remain poor readers, they have missed out on an enormous amount of text exposure and reading practice compared to average readers. By one estimate, the number of words read by a middle-school student who is a good reader approaches one million compared with 100,000 for a poor reader. In other words, reading failure seems to compound learning failure exponentially with every grade year passed. This difference places poor readers at a significant disadvantage with respect to vocabulary development, sight word development, and the development of reading fluency. In short, reading becomes an onerous chore, a chore that is frequently avoided.

Fourth, and related to the above, the assessment and identification practices employed today under the existing definition of LD and the accompanying requirements of IDEA work directly against identifying children with LD before the second or even the third grade. Specifically, as Dr. Pasternack explained, the over reliance on the use of the IQ-achievement discrepancy criterion for the identification of LD means that a child must fail or fall below a predicted level of performance before he or she is eligible for special education services. Because achievement failure sufficient to produce a discrepancy from IQ cannot be reliably measured until a child reaches approximately nine years of age, the use of the IQ-achievement discrepancy literally constitutes a "wait to fail"

model. Thus the youngster has suffered the academic and emotional strains of failure for two or three years or even more before potentially effective specialized instruction can be brought to bear. Thus, it is not surprising that our NICHD longitudinal data show clearly that the majority of children who are poor readers at age nine or older continue to have reading difficulties into adulthood.
In summary, the increase in the incidence of LD over the past quarter century are not solely due to improved identification of learning disabilities. Rather, the increases in identification, particularly within the older age ranges, reflect the fact that Federal policy as set out in the IDEA led to ineffective, inaccurate and frequently invalid identification practices to continue placing highly vulnerable children at further risk

Explanations for Why Special Education Services Are Not Effective in Improving Learning and Achievement

There are two major reasons why traditional models of special education service provision have proven ineffective. First, the standard "specialized" instruction provided through typical remediation models is frequently too little, too general, and too unsystematic. For example, Sharon Vaughn and her colleagues, with support from OSEP, studied children with LD in reading who were served for an entire year in public elementary school special education resource rooms. They found that the "special education" was characterized primarily by whole group reading instruction provided to large groups of children (5 to 19) who also varied widely in grade level (grades 3-5). Despite this variation, little individualized or differentiated instruction occurred. The results of this study converge with several other studies identifying the same ineffective practices.

Second, and related to an issue discussed earlier, even if the instruction were of high quality, it may be too late to have maximal benefits given that students with LD placed in special education classrooms are already woefully far behind and less motivated to learn to read following one, two, or three years of failure.

It Does Not Have to Be This Way

The best mainstream scientific research supported by the NICHD and OSEP – studies that reflect the consensus of experts in such fields as special education, general education, child development, psychology and the neurosciences – indicates that most longstanding differences in defining and educating students with LD stem from inaccurate assumptions about the causes and characteristics of LD. Moreover, there is compelling and converging evidence from these fields that justifies investments in early identification and prevention programs for children at risk for LD. This is especially effective with LD in reading, which is a common and troublesome type of LD, constituting 80 to 90 percent of all students with LD. Fortunately, reading disabilities are also the best understood and most effectively corrected learning difficulty under certain conditions, if identified and addressed early.

There is evidence that if children receive effective instruction early and intensively, they can often make large gains in general academic achievement. Indeed, in early intervention and prevention studies supported by the NICHD and OSEP, reading failure rates as high as 38 to 40 percent can be reduced to six percent or less. And, as Assistant Secretary Pasternack pointed out, by reducing reading failure in the majority of students who would fail without proper early intervention, special education resources can now be deployed intensively and with greater provision to that six percent of struggling readers who did not respond to early intervention.

We now have substantial scientific evidence that early intervention can greatly reduce the number of older children who are identified as LD. Without early identification and the provision of effective early intervention, children with LD, as well as other students with reading difficulties, will require long-term, intensive and expensive special education programs, many of which continue to show meager results. Early intervention allows ineffective remedial programs to be replaced with effective prevention, while providing older students who continue to need specialized services with highly informed and evidenced-based intensive instruction so they can return as quickly as possible to the educational mainstream. This should be the primary focus of special education for students with LD – the instruction of those children who continue to suffer failure in reading, mathematics, and written language despite well-documented and systematic early instruction.

Recommendations

There are few areas where the relationship of science and policy are more loosely linked than in the area of learning disabilities. In too many instances, policy-related issues have driven the scientific agenda relevant to LD. The situation should be reversed; scientific research should inform policies that address LD. But the production of clear, convergent scientific findings is only the first step. Effecting meaningful change in the lives of children and teachers requires that we not only have sound scientific findings, but that we understand how to formulate policies based on these findings to produce changes at the individual child level.

While it is clear that we now have overwhelming evidence that changes are needed in the LD identification and service provision areas, we must expect and anticipate unintended consequences that may follow any changes in current legislative language. I realize that even the best evidence-based recommendations will not be utilized and sustained in practice unless careful thought is given to identifying the conditions that will increase the probability of their successful implementation.

These conditions include our ability to: (1) ensure that all recommendations have been sufficiently tested to acknowledge clearly their strengths and weaknesses and evaluate their specific impact on the children and adults to be served; (2) ensure that all programs that are implemented on the basis of policy are based upon the highest quality of scientific evidence and are continuously evaluated for the efficacy; (3) ensure that all policies and programs are held to the highest levels of accountability and linked explicitly

to documented improvements in student achievement; (4) anticipate the effects of changes in policies and practices on federal, state, and local communities and address them effectively; (5) take into account barriers to change in public school policy and practice; and (6) articulate specific areas where capacity must be developed to ensure successful implementation.
Within the context of these general recommendations, the following specific recommendations are provided:

(1) Replace the exclusionary definition which identifies LD on the basis of what it is not with evidence-based inclusionary definitions that specify clearly what it is. These definitions must specify and distinguish disabilities in reading, mathematics, written expression, and oral language.

(2) Discontinue the use of the IQ-achievement discrepancy criterion in the identification of LD. This will require validated alternatives. For example, in most cases, particularly in reading, student underachievement can be predicted on the basis of performance on measures assessing skills directly related to the academic domain in question. In addition, underachievement can be documented by direct comparisons of students' age and grade with their academic functioning in oral language, reading, writing, and mathematics.

(3) Include a student's response to well-designed and well implemented early intervention as part of the identification process for LD. There is a pressing need for early, intensive, empirically based interventions to be made easily available to children through general education. No doubt, children who do not benefit from these interventions will require more intensive remediation programs as well as educational accommodations as they proceed through school. In essence, the identification of LD would be reserved for children whose reading and other academic deficits appear to be severe and intractable. This would allow them to receive more comprehensive and intensive help earlier and with greater focus. In turn, this would prompt researchers to more intensive study to determine how the environment, the brain, and heredity interact to impede response to early instruction. This is by no means an attempt to "write off" children who do not respond to aggressive early instruction. To the contrary, it is an attempt to maximize their learning potential through scientifically sound and effective practices.

(4) Related to number 3, ensure that the development and implementation of early identification, prevention and early intervention programs are the joint responsibility of both regular and special education.

(5) Related to number 4, acknowledge the limitations of current teacher preparation programs and models for both general and special educators. The statement that many children are identified as LD are actually "instructional casualties" is unfortunately all too often accurate. Almost all children can learn to read, for example, if taught appropriately, but many miss out on the help they need

because teachers are not adequately prepared. Both special and general educators must be prepared on the basis of the converging scientific evidence of how children learn, why some children have difficulties, and how the most effective instructional approaches can be identified and implemented. All educators should share a common language about these fundamental principles and hold a common dedication and ability to address the needs of students who arrive in their classrooms from highly diverse backgrounds and a range of initial abilities. To do this, we must help teachers to identify the characteristics of high quality research and to be able to distinguish between research that is trustworthy and that which is weak and ill-informed.

(6) Encourage alternative models for teacher preparation and continuing professional development. Teachers must be provided the critical academic content, pedagogical principles, and knowledge of learner characteristics that they need in order to impart evidence-based systematic and informed instruction to their students.

An Example of Translating Scientific Research into Practice

Attached to my testimony are additional materials that describe and document how the recommendations noted above can be implemented with success in real schools and real classrooms. I offer for the record a description of how the effectiveness of reading instruction was significantly improved and led to substantial improvements in student reading achievement in this particular school. The research conducted in this school is an example of comparable research efforts in 12 additional early reading intervention research sites supported by the NICHD, all showing similar improvements in reading following the implementation of scientifically-based reading instruction. The attached paper that provides this information was written by Ray King, principal of the Hartsfield Elementary School in Tallahassee, Florida and by Dr. Joe Torgesen, one of the leading reading researchers in the country and an NICHD researcher. As I provide an overview of the study, I would like to draw your attention to the figures on page 14 of the paper, which denotes changes in the end-of-year reading performance of children as a function of the implementation of scientifically based early intervention.

Over a five-year period, Hartsfield Elementary School worked to implement a comprehensive reading curriculum in kindergarten through grade 3, and to establish significant amounts of preventive reading instruction for children who were performing significantly below grade level in the first and second grade. The school serves a population of children who are about 60 percent minority and 60 percent of the students are eligible for free or reduced lunch support. In the first year of the program, the new classroom reading instruction was only partially implemented in all primary grade classrooms. The preventive instruction was phased in gradually beginning in the second year of the project as new resources for providing the instruction were identified. The test used to measure reading skills was a nationally standardized measure of word reading abilities, and it was given to the students at the end of each year by individuals other than the children's teachers. The figures show the percentage of children who ended first and second grade performing below the 25th percentile, and it also describes the change in average percentile for all children. As you can see in the top figure, during the five-year implementation period, the percentage of children performing below the 25th percentile at the end of the first grade dropped from 31.8 percent to 3.7 percent. Likewise, during the five-year implementation period, the percentage of children performing below the 25th percentile at the end of the second grade was only 2.4 percent. In terms of long-term impact of early intervention at Hartsfield Elementary, during the same period of time, the school achieved the largest growth of any of the 20 elementary schools in the district on the state-administered reading test given at the end of the third grade. Moreover, during the project period, the average Metropolitan Reaching Achievement Test scores for the entire third grade increased from the 49th percentile to the 73rd percentile because of the reading improvement observed among the school's lowest performing students.

I would also like to draw your attention to the figure in the second attachment that you also have that depicts what occurs in a youngster's brain when that child learns to read through the provision of scientifically-based reading instruction provided by well trained teachers. You will note on the top right side of the figure a left hemisphere of an at-risk reader participating in a NICHD study directed by Dr. Jack Fletcher at the University of Texas Health Science Center in Houston. Dr. Fletcher and his associates were able to identify this child as at risk for reading failure early and then provided intensive and comprehensive reading instruction to improve reading skills. At the end of 65 hours of instruction, this child is now reading at the average level and his improved reading abilities are mirrored in increases in brain activity in those neural systems responsible for reading. This is one example of how positive changes in reading outcomes are mirrored by changes in brain activation. We see that effective early instruction can not only help a child learn to read, but also may induce changes in the brain to mirror normalized levels of activation.

In closing, we have learned a great deal over the past twenty-five years about how children learn and why some of those youngsters experience difficulties. We have learned a tremendous amount about reading development and reading disabilities and are confident that we can ensure that all but two to six percent of children can become successful readers under the proper assessment and instructional conditions.

Thank you Mr. Chairman, and I would be happy to answer any questions that you or members of the Subcommittee may have.

Attachment 1 to Dr. Lyon's Testimony

Improving the Effectiveness of Reading Instruction in One Elementary School: A Description of the Process

Ray King
Hartsfield Elementary School

Joseph K. Torgesen
Florida State University

We wish to thank all the school personnel at Hartsfield Elementary School who have contributed so importantly to the changes described in this article. We also wish to thank the parents and members of the community who have served on the School Advisory Boards that have provided both vision and focus for this effort.

This article provides a partial description of a whole school change project that has taken place over the last four years at Hartsfield Elementary School in Tallahassee, Florida. The primary focus of the article is on reading instruction and achievement. This is a partial report in that many variables contributed to the success of the reading program, and only a few of them are described here. Some of the variables that will not be considered in detail are: a) changes in teacher and parent attitudes contributing to significant changes in school culture; b) increased parent and teacher expectations for behavior and academic performance; c) substantive changes in personnel and the roles of certain staff; d) expansion of pre-kindergarten programs; and, e) the district's commitment to site-based decision making at the school level.

The six key elements that will be addressed in this article, and that we consider critical to the gains in reading achievement we have experienced over the past four years, are:

- commitment to meeting individual student needs at all levels;
- adopting and implementing a research-based reading curriculum;
- objective assessment to evaluate student progress and the effectiveness of reading programs;
- designing and implementing an effective instructional delivery system;
- maximizing available instructional time and
- administrative monitoring of student progress and program implementation;
-

Description of School Before Change Process Began

Demographics

Hartsfield has evolved over the last 10 years from a school that was predominantly white and middle-class to a school with an almost 60% free/reduced lunch enrollment and a 60% minority (predominantly African-American) student body. Five years ago the free-reduced lunch rate was 46% . The middle-class neighborhoods in our zone were aging and fewer families were moving into these areas. At the same time, the size and number of families in the public housing neighborhoods located in the zone continued to increase. Teachers accustomed to teaching middle-class children were not prepared for the increasing instructional demands associated with the changing characteristics of our students.

School Culture Regarding Reading

The overall attitude among staff was one of providing the content and letting students who could learn do so while others continued to fall academically further behind. There was a wide range of academic abilities in the classrooms. For example, some kindergarten students entered school able to read many familiar words and also able to "sound out" simple unknown words, while others did not know one letter of the alphabet and could not distinguish letters from numbers. Our situation precisely reflected the difficulties noted in Olson's (1998) recent observation that a central problem in reading instruction arises, not from the absolute level of children's preparation for learning to read, but from the diversity in their levels of preparation.

In our school at this time, there was little variation in the curriculum to address the varied reading needs of students. Students academically behind did not receive the focused, intensive instruction necessary for their success. Instead, teachers developed a culture of acceptance of failure for these students, blaming the home and lack of parental support.

Students falling behind were referred to special education or Chapter I programs and sent to "pull-out" resource classrooms. The resource teachers in these classrooms were expected to address the needs of these students. As a result, there was no sense of ownership by the regular classroom teachers for these students' achievement. Little was done, except in a few classrooms, to address reading deficits within the regular classroom reading curriculum. In addition, more academically able students were not challenged in the regular classroom since teachers taught "to the middle". As a result, both the middle-class and less advantaged students did not receive effective instruction geared to their reading levels.

Curriculum Organization

At this point in time, curriculum and textbooks in reading were adopted at the district level. Schools generally went along with the adoption with some degree of flexibility at the school level. Kindergarten through fifth grades were expected to teach the traditional curriculum areas of language arts, math, social studies, science, art, music and physical education. Although the district had adopted texts, their use varied within a school and even within grade levels at a school. Hartsfield Elementary was an excellent example of curriculum variability within a school and among teachers at a grade level.

There was little curriculum coordination among teachers at a grade level except in a few instances where teachers adopted a common "theme". These instructional themes could involve dinosaurs, sea life, or some other topic. This same theme could appear the next year with the next grade level's teacher. In some instances, students received the same theme for three consecutive years. Also, some teachers used the adopted language arts text to teach reading while others used no textbook at all and simply pulled instruction from "a variety of resources". Hence, there was no reading program except the adopted reading series which was sporadically used in the school. Students at a certain grade level were exposed to whatever skills or content a teacher chose to use in her/his class. At the end of the year, with the exception of district wide achievement testing, there was no assessment of reading skills to provide information to next year's teacher. Additionally, there was no on-going reading assessment in the classrooms.

Instructional Delivery

Instructional delivery was very "departmentalized" at the school. The "departments" consisted of learning disabilities, speech/language, and Chapter I services. Coordination was rare among the teachers in grade levels, Chapter I, and special education .

"Pull-out" programs were the sole instructional delivery system for students with learning disabilities, speech and language deficits, and those qualified for Chapter I (now Title I) services. There was little communication about reading strategies and curriculum approaches since there was not a school-wide curriculum for reading at Hartsfield. This meant a classroom teacher might use a phonics approach while a resource teacher used whole language strategies. Since there was no assessment or coordination of instruction, accountability for student learning was non-existent. Students receiving these pull-out services experienced what Slavin and Madden (1989) term "cognitive confusion" created by multiple instructional approaches to reading.

The problem was made worse by the fact that students needing additional learning time spent much of their day in "transition", walking the corridors from their classrooms to speech, to Chapter I, finally returning to their classrooms. A great deal of instructional time was lost in travel as well as at transitional points among classrooms. Regular classroom teachers were concerned that they rarely had the whole class intact, due to constant "pull-out" time for certain students. Also, due to the "departmentalized" approach, there was not a focus on the most pressing needs of an individual student. Instead, each classroom teacher and resource teacher was operating independently and not considering individual student priorities. The primary need for most of these students was learning to read. Despite this need, many spent extra instructional time in mathematics and continued to fall further behind in reading.

Special area services for art, music and physical education were scheduled so they did not occur at the same time every day for all teachers at the same grade level. This meant that one first grade teacher would receive physical education on Tuesday at 9:00 while another received music at 9:30. The blocks of time for special area services were also varied during the week from 30 to 60 minutes per day. Although there were some days with common special area times for a specific grade level, it did not occur on a daily basis. This scheduling arrangement created frequent noise in the corridors and no constant planning times for grade level teachers.

Student Achievement

The California Achievement Test (CATV) is the group administered, standardized assessment used in our district to assess student progress. The CATV was administered to third through fifth grades in the spring of 1993 and 1994. The average median percentile score for children in 3rd, 4th, and 5th, grades for the 1993 and 1994 school years was 50, 52, and 48. Although these figures placed our children close to the national average in terms of overall performance, far too many of our students were performing from 1.5 to 2 grade levels below their current grade placement. Poor reading skills were interfering with many children's progress through the curriculum in third, fourth, and fifth grades, and these children were also not prepared to move into the middle school curriculum after leaving Hartsfield.

Preparation for Change - Deciding the Direction

During the 1993-94 school year, there were a series of meetings among parents, teachers and the administration. The School Advisory Council comprised of parents and teachers and the Parent Teacher Organization (PTO) met together to discuss concerns regarding student discipline and academic achievement. We worked collaboratively on a series of belief statements and a school vision which emphasized student responsibility and student achievement. It was unanimously adopted by parents. The faculty and administration met together, sometimes with parents sometimes without, to discuss the vision and belief statements and identify strategies to begin moving in a desired direction. The faculty, after much discussion and two inservice sessions discussing reading research, identified our two primary problems. First, students were not prepared to enter kindergarten, and second, we had no consistent reading program at Hartsfield. The first problem was addressed by expanding the pre-kindergarten program through constructing an infant-toddler wing on the school (supported by a $470,000 grant) and doubling the size of our early childhood program. The second area, lack of a consistent reading program, was our core problem. We had now, as a faculty, admitted we had the problem, which was the first step to solving it.

The Change Process: School Year 1993-94

Change in the Instructional Delivery System

In 1993-94, teachers expressed the concern that they needed more time to plan together to insure more consistent content and instructional strategies at the grade levels. Also, they expressed frustration at our "helter skelter" schedule of pulling students out of their classes for resource assistance. Some teachers had their entire class together for less than one hour per day. One part of the solution to these problems involved block scheduling for special area (art, music, physical education, and media) programs.

This allowed, for instance, all of the second grade classes to attend a special area for the same 45 minute period every day, enabling teachers to share common planning times. In addition, we moved all of our primary classes special area times to after lunch. This allowed these classes large blocks of instructional time during the mornings, a prime learning time for younger children. Third through fifth grades had 75-90 minutes of uninterrupted periods in the morning and the same in the afternoons, while primary had 180 uninterrupted instructional minutes in the mornings and 45 in the afternoons.

In order to address the concern regarding the constant pulling of students from their regular classrooms, we began a team-teaching approach piloted the year before in a fifth and fourth grade classroom. The team-teaching approach meant the resource teacher came to the classroom instead of pulling groups of students from the class. While the rest of the children were receiving reading instruction in groups from the classroom teacher or working at centers, the children with learning disabilities received small group instruction from the resource teacher. We adopted this service delivery system for students with learning disabilities (LD) in grades one through five in our school.

This practice required us to "cluster" our LD and language impaired students in certain classrooms, but it had several important benefits. It eliminated student travel time to resource rooms, reduced the number of transitions between classrooms, and saved instructional time. This increased the total amount of instructional time during the day for our academically needy students. We also noticed another significant benefit associated with this service delivery system. It created interaction between the regular and resource teachers and fostered consistent instructional approaches for all students. Also, students who did not quite qualify for special programs and who traditionally "fell through the cracks", began receiving the individualized small group instruction necessary for their academic progress. They were frequently included with the special needs students since their curricular needs were similar. This resulted in regular and special education students receiving instruction at their academic level.

The reading curriculum

After reviewing research on reading and reading instruction with Dr. Joseph Torgesen, and our faculty, we focused on two commercially available reading programs. One was Open Court Publishing's *Collections for Young Scholars* (Open Court Reading, 1995) and the other was Science Research Associates' *Reading Mastery* (Englemann & Bruner, 1995)) program. At this time, our special education resource and Chapter I teachers were using the SRA Reading Mastery program with our students with learning disabilities and some Chapter I students at all grade levels, and they strongly supported this approach. Our K-2 teachers were sent to observe these programs and we reviewed research and materials and invited representatives from the two publishers as well as teachers who had used these programs to speak with us about their success.

The Open Court curriculum presents a balance of phonemic awareness, phonics (with blending as a key strategy), and literature activities. The program teaches phonetic elements using sound-spelling cards, alliterative stories, and controlled vocabulary texts that practice the rule just taught. A parallel strand uses Big Books story sharing activities to promote oral language comprehension and love of literature. We had studied the summary of *Beginning to Read: Thinking and Learning about Print* (Stahl, Osborn, & Lehr, 1990) and were pleased to note that Marilyn Adams, the author of the work from which this summary was made (Adams, 1990), was a senior author on the Open Court reading curriculum.

The Change Process: School Year 1994-1995

Changes to the basic reading curriculum

For the 1994-95 school year, we included the adoption of Open Court's *Collections for Young Scholars* in our school improvement plan for kindergarten through second grades. We also decided to continue the SRA *Reading Mastery* curriculum with our third, fourth and fifth grade students with learning disabilities and some Chapter I students in second grade.

Kindergarten through second grade and resource teachers attended a three day inservice for Open Court during the summer and the consultant came to the school to assist with beginning the program in our kindergarten through second grade classrooms. The consultant returned every three to four weeks during the first semester and met with the grade level teachers. One problem with the initial inservice was that it should have been more explicit regarding the importance of addressing the key components of the Open Court lesson on a daily basis. Teachers thought, and justifiably so, they could select some components of the lesson and not use others. In addition, there was some resistance among several teachers on the basis that they were being "forced" to teach in a way that was inconsistent with their "philosophy" of reading while others simply were not able to provide adequate instruction. For these reasons, the implementation was "uneven" within grade levels with some teachers fully implementing the program and others inconsistently using parts of the program.

The Change Process: 1995-96

For the 1995-96 year, we continued our special area block scheduling and committed ourselves to significant changes through the school improvement plan process. These included:

1) requiring by written expectation and discussion in team meetings as well as frequent administrative observations in the classroom the use of the Open Court curriculum in kindergarten through second grades;
2) eliminating all "pull-out" resource times except speech articulation;
3) completing the adoption of the SRA *Reading Mastery* Program in third, fourth and fifth grades for all students;
4) initiating small group reading instruction for all students in all grades;
5) suspending the social studies and some math curriculum in first and

second grade.

6) using reading subtests from the Woodcock-Johnson Psycho-Educational Battery-Revised (Woodcock & Johnson, 1989) to individually evaluate the reading level of all first and second grade students.

All of these changes were addressed directly or indirectly in our school improvement plan for 1995-96. We used a small writing team and frequent meetings among teachers and administration in grade level groups to discuss the research and proposed curriculum changes. A parent from our School Advisory Council was on the school improvement plan writing team.

Administrative support actions and curriculum changes

Once discussed and written in the plan, all staff understood it was the administration's responsibility to insure the plan was effectively implemented at the school. There was a faculty meeting and a series of grade level team meetings which continued throughout the year. The expectation regarding curriculum and instructional delivery changes were outlined in detail and the teachers were involved at every step in the scheduling, assessment, and implementation of programs. It was also clear that the implementation was a major consideration in the administration's evaluation of teacher performance.

The adoption of the SRA Reading Mastery Program for all third through fifth grade students meant a commitment to teacher inservice and expenditure of school dollars to purchase materials and supplies to run the program. This step insured extra help for students below grade level and advanced instruction for more academically able students. Once begun, there was a need for periodic monitoring of the program to insure students were instructed at the correct reading levels There was also some resistance in terms of teacher's philosophical differences regarding the grouping of students for instruction. This was similar to what occurred when Open Court began in the lower grades. These inconsistencies throughout the first year of SRA in all of the upper grades made the program less effective.

At the mid-year point, we noticed that a substantial number of our second graders were still struggling with beginning reading skills in the area of phonetic decoding (being able to "sound out" novel words in text). For these children, we began using SRA Fast Cycle (a combination of Reading Mastery I and II) in their small group instruction. By the end of the year, we noticed a marked change in their word attack skills, although some students learned at a much slower rate and required more repetition.

Further changes in instructional delivery

Eliminating all "pull-out" programs except speech articulation required a great deal of preparation and teacher cooperation. We began the previous Spring by loading classes with approximately the same number of students at each academic level. In other words, in every class we attempted to have equal numbers of students with high, average and below average reading skills. We did not at this point have reliable assessment results and were using the CATV for grades 3-5 , Marie Clay's (1995) *Concepts of Print* test for kindergarten, and teacher judgments to make these decisions. Our purpose in using the assessment information for class loading was to insure enough students at a given academic level were assigned to each class to form an instructional group for that class. We did assign all of our language impaired and LD students in two classes per grade level. The other class or classes received "border line" students with similar academic needs who did not quite qualify for a special program. We continued to form self-contained classes for students with moderate to severe mental handicaps and behavioral disabilities.

In order to initiate small group instruction, we clustered small groups of three to six students according to reading levels in each first through fifth grade class. We then scheduled each resource teacher to be in a classroom for 75 to 90 minutes per day. This meant the resource teachers were seeing three to four classrooms per day and teaching two to three reading groups per class. Some classes received a trained paraprofessional to run reading groups. Paraprofessionals, as long as they received periodic inservice and were monitored, were as effective as teachers using the SRA program. Decisions on when to move students among reading groups resided with the resource and classroom teachers. The resource positions were funded from special education and Chapter I funds.

The regular teacher saw two to three reading groups while the resource teacher was in the room. The other students not in a group were assigned seat work and rotated into a reading group during the resource teacher's time in their class. This captured a great deal of instructional time since it eliminated student movement outside the classrooms.

Teachers were concerned about the large amount of instructional time used in kindergarten through second grades to implement the Open Court Program. We agreed to eliminate classroom science and social studies and some math for the year. This enabled our primary teachers to focus on the reading and writing curriculum for their students.

Assessment of Reading Skill

At the beginning of the 1995-96 school year, we began assessing reading levels using the Word Attack and Word Identification subtests from the Woodcock-Johnson Psycho-Educational Battery-Revised. These assessments were administered to all first and second grade students within the first three weeks of school. We had trained our resource teachers and guidance counselor to administer the assessment. We also decided that the resource teachers would not administer the test to students they would be teaching during the year. The classroom teachers were not involved in the test administration other than providing blocks of times for the resource teachers to test students. This testing arrangement increased the reliability of our results. The resource teachers and guidance teacher used this same procedure at the end of the year. We used the results to assess individual student progress for the year and the aggregate data to evaluate the effectiveness of our reading program in first and second grades. We continued the individual assessment of kindergarten students but changed from the *Concepts of Print* assessment to the *Bracken Basic Concept Scale (Bracken, 1984).*

The usefulness of our individual reading assessments for documenting the effectiveness of the changes we made to our reading curriculum is illustrated in Figure 1. In this graph, we have plotted the number of children in first and second grade who had word reading skills below the

----

Insert Figure 1 about here

25th percentile at different points in time. Among children in first grade, the percent of children with word reading skills below the 25th percentile dropped from 31.8 at the end of the 1994-95 school year to 3.7 at the end of the 1998-1999 year. During the same period, the average percentile of first grade children rose from 48.9 to 82. Children in second grade were not tested at the end of the 1994-95 school year,, but achievement has generally been stronger as children have been in the program longer. During this same period of time, the median percentile in reading achievement for our third grade children on the California Achievement Test jumped from 49 at the end of 1994 to 73 at the end of 1999.

The Change Process: 1996-97

We continued to use the school improvement plan process to plot our course of action. For the 1996-97 school year we focused on the following:

1) continuing our direction begun the previous year - clear expectations regarding implementation of curriculum; scheduling to increase instructional time, team-teaching approach in all classrooms, small group instruction and objective assessment of student progress;
2) emphasizing changes at the kindergarten level to include assessment and programmatic changes for language and phonemic awareness to intervene with our youngest students;
3) initiating a six week summer program for our "at risk" four year olds preparing to enter kindergarten;
(4) initiating a pre/post test (Bracken Basic Concept Scale) for pre-k students;
5) implementing *Accelerated Reader* (1994) a reading and computer assisted instruction and assessment program as a supplement to our basic reading curriculum and
6) initiating a "home reading" program for kindergarten through third grades.

Administrative support actions

It is important to emphasize that the commitment to previous year's changes and the will to continue those improvements needed to be continuously supported through planned administrative/leadership actions. These actions were accomplished primarily through faculty and grade level meetings as well as one-to-one discussions with teachers. Many of our earlier changes were infrastructure type changes. These included an emphasis on uninterrupted classroom instruction, increased instructional time resulting from master schedule changes, elimination of pull-out programs and other measures outlined earlier. The point here is that these types of changes can be degraded and undermined if teachers and staff are not continuously reminded of the vision statements that guided these changes in the first place. Further, individual teachers frequently require help in solving problems that arise from these scheduling constraints so that whatever adaptations are made do not undermine the overall effectiveness of the instructional delivery system.

Further changes to the reading curriculum

The individual reading assessment program we began using the previous year showed us that many children were still leaving second grade unprepared for third grade level work in reading. In the previous year, we had begun using the SRA Fast Cycle Reading program with our lower performing children beginning in the second semester of second grade. For the six weeks of summer school, we began to provide many of these children with two reading sessions per day using the SRA program. This provided our these students with a preview and some experience with the SRA Reading program, in addition to adding further substantial gains to their basic word reading ability. Unfortunately, some of our students continued to struggle in the Fast Cycle Program.

At the same time that we were attempting to strengthen reading instruction for children with the weakest skills, the use of small group instruction was working very well to challenge our students with the strongest reading skills. At the end of the fourth grade, we had 20 of 74 students in a Level VI, grade six reading program. We also decided to add the *Accelerated Reader* (1994) program for all of our students in third, fourth and fifth grades. The *Accelerated Reader* program is basically a way of monitoring children's outside-of-class reading so they can be encouraged and rewarded for doing more reading outside of assigned class materials. We began offering incentive awards to encourage students to read. As students read books, they took a computerized test on the content of the book. The software in the *Accelerated Reader* program keeps a running record of all books read and the score of each comprehension test. By the second semester, we had second and first grade teachers also using the program and requesting more books on their students' levels. We purchased additional disks and books for kindergarten through second grades.

One of our major concerns and an initial reason for beginning the *Accelerated Reader* program was reading fluency. Although we work on fluency with students in SRA, there was an overall concern among the faculty that we needed something that involved our parents in reading. As Cunningham & Stanovich (1998) have recently underlined, once children acquire beginning reading skills, one of the keys to their becoming good readers by the end of elementary school is wide exposure to text. Thus, we began the read-at-home program for kindergarten through third grades.

We used out-of-adoption reading series books to send home with our children. The parents signed off on the pages read nightly. This was very successful at two grade levels and had an inconsistent implementation in two others. It did improve the fluency for some students and was a great way to involve parents in their children's' education.

Changes at the Kindergarten Level

At the beginning of the second semester of this school year, we administered the *Test of Phonological Awareness* (TOPA) (Torgesen & Bryant, 1994) to all of our kindergarten children. Using this test, we identified students with severe weaknesses in phonological awareness. For these children, we initiated small group DISTAR language lessons (Engelmann & Osborn, 1987) in 20 minute sessions four days per week . We assessed these kindergarten students with the *Bracken Basic Concept Scale* at the end of the year to evaluate student progress and determine those needing to attend summer school.

Most of the children needed to attend. At the conclusion of summer school, we assessed kindergarten students to determine those needing the extra assistance in first grade. Four of the 18 students attending summer school went into the regular Open Court curriculum in 1997-98, while the others participated in small group instruction using the SRA *Reading Mastery I* curriculum. We felt that the SRA curriculum was more properly paced for these weaker students, and also that it provided more opportunities for explicit practice and skill building than did the *Collections for Young Scholars* materials. Those students receiving SRA also received the benefits of a portion of the Open Court lessons as well.

The Change Process: 1997-98

For 1997-98, we identified some additional instructional strategies to make our students more successful. These included:
1) continuing to emphasize and monitor implementation of Open Court, SRA and *Accelerated Reader* programs;
2) provide small group instruction to our weakest first and second grade children using the Reading Mastery Curriculum (using Reading Mastery I and II instead of Fast Cycle) rather than the Open Court curriculum;
3) implement the *Standardized Test of Assessment for Reading* (1995) (STAR) to determine leisure reading levels of students;
4) implement the *Waterford Reading Program*, Level 1 (Waterford Institute, 1995) in kindergarten and one first grade classroom; and,
5) expanding instruction for language delayed kindergarten students.

Further changes to the reading curriculum

We were convinced at this point that there was conclusive research to suggest the importance of explicit phonics instruction for less advantaged children (Brown & Felton, 1990; Foorman, Francis, Fletcher, Schatschneider, & Mehta, 1998). Although this type of instruction is provided in the Open Court curriculum, and some of our students from low income families were successful with it, many were not making adequate progress. As mentioned previously, we used the summer school data to determine which students needed SRA in first grade. Beginning this year, these students received their small group instruction using the *Reading Mastery* curriculum.

Continuing Administrative Support Actions

The principal, assistant principal, and an SRA trainer monitor the reading programs at all grade levels. One critical area to monitor is student's oral reading performance. Oral reading provides critical insight into the way children are progressing with both the accuracy and fluency of their word reading skills. Since all of our students read in small groups daily, this is easy to accomplish. In some rooms, the teachers were grading the daily, written comprehension assignments but not the actual reading. We met with the teachers, outlined the problem and talked with them about the solution. It was rectified within the week and is periodically monitored through observations. We use this as an example of what may happen if the principal and assistant principal are not actively involved in the reading program to help keep the attention of all personnel focused on the reading goals and achievements that everyone has agreed are important.

Assessment of Reading Skills

We began the *Standardized Test of Assessment for Reading* (STAR) (1995) this year. Using the STAR software, we evaluate the leisure and instructional reading level for each student. All students reading at the school take the assessment on a quarterly basis. This includes kindergarten children who are reading. In addition to generating individualized reading levels, it also produces a parent report and maintains a record of the results for each student. In addition, all students registering are assessed using the *Bracken* (kindergarten), *Woodcock-Johnson*(1st and 2nd grades) or SRA placement (3rd, 4th and 5th grades).

Additions to the kindergarten curriculum

Given the large diversity in preparation for reading of the children coming into Hartsfield, we felt the need to continue to improve the quality of important pre-reading skills at this level. One strategy we adopted to provide high quality, individualized instruction in concepts about print, letter knowledge, phonological awareness, and vocabulary was to implement the *Waterford Early Reading Program*, Level 1, in our kindergarten classrooms. This program is extremely engaging for young children, and it provides 20 minutes of individualized, high quality computer based instruction every day for the entire kindergarten year. An additional attractive feature of the program is that it has a set of books and video tapes which go home with the parents to use with their children.

In addition, we continue to provide small group instruction using the DISTAR (Engelmann & Osborn, 1987) language curriculum. This year, we added an additional 10 to 15 min. per day of specific instruction in phonemic awareness using activities from *Phonemic Awareness in Young Children: A Classroom Curriculum* that has been developed by Adams, Foorman, Lundberg, and Beeler (1997).

Concluding comments

The recent comprehensive report on the prevention of reading problems in young children published by the National Research Council (Snow, Burns, & Griffin, 1998), suggests that the first step toward insuring that all children acquire effective reading skills involves a sound basic reading curriculum in kindergarten through second grade. We would agree with that statement, but we would also emphasize that schools must be prepared to go substantially beyond that step in order to reach all of their children. In our estimation the most important of these additional steps are: 1) identification of resources and procedures for delivering effective small group or individual instruction to higher risk children beginning in kindergarten and extending at least through second grade; 2) regular assessment of early reading growth to insure that the needs of all children are being met; 3) continuing administrative leadership to insure proper coordination and execution of all elements of the preventive effort; and, 4) a realistic time frame for implementation of all elements of the overall program.

Even though the reading achievement of children in first and second grades at Hartsfield Elementary School has shown substantial improvement over the last four years, we recognize that there are still many ways we can continue to improve our support of reading growth in our children. We are currently planning efforts for two initiatives to help many of our children enter kindergarten more prepared to learn to read and succeed in school. In our school based pre-K programs, we are beginning to institute a developmentally appropriate curriculum that will more systematically support the acquisition of pre-reading skills such as vocabulary, print awareness, and sensitivity to the sound structure of language. In coordination with these school-based experiences, we are also anxious to work with the Pre-K Parent/Teacher Organization to more effectively increase parental awareness concerning home based activities that can support growth in emergent literacy skills.

In addition to these improvements at the Pre-K level, we are currently planning for continuing efforts in the K-5 program in three areas. First we are investigating ways to more effectively use computer assisted instruction and practice to support reading growth at all grade levels. We view computer technology as particularly effective in providing the structured and motivating practice that many of our children require to consolidate the skills they are taught in the classroom. Second, we recognize the need for more teacher training focused on the "higher order" thinking skills that are required in the development of high levels of literacy. Our work thus far has focused primarily on word level reading skills, and now we must begin to explore ways to expand our efforts in helping our children develop the language and thinking skills required for high level comprehension of text. Finally, we recognize that we must continue to focus on recruitment of high quality teachers who share our philosophical and research based orientation to reading instruction for all children. If we can accomplish these goals over the next five years, we expect to come very close to the ideal of assisting all children to acquire the reading skills required succeed at the next level of their education.

References

Accelerated Reader (1994). Wisconsin Rapids, WI: Advantage Learning Systems, Inc.

Adams, M.J.(1990). *Beginning to read: Thinking and learning about print.* Cambridge, MA: MIT Press.

Adams, M. J., Foorman, B.R., Lundberg, I., Beeler, T. (1997). *Phonemic awareness in young children: A classroom curriculum.* Baltimore, MD: Brooks Publishing.

Bracken, B.A. (1984). *Bracken Basic Concept Scale.* San Antonio: The Psychological Corporation.

Brown, I. S. & Felton, R. H. (1990) Effects of instruction on beginning reading skills in children at risk for reading disability. *Reading and Writing: An Interdisciplinary Journal, 2*, 223-241.

Cunningham, A.E. & Stanovich, K.E. (1998). What reading does for the mind. *American Educator, 22*, 8-15.

Clay, M. M. (1985). *The early detection of reading difficulties.* Portsmouth, NH: Heinemann.

Englemann, S., & Bruner, E.C. (1995). *SRA Reading Mastery Rainbow Edition.* Chicago, IL: SRA/McGraw-Hill.

Englemann, S., & Osborn, J. (1987). *DISTAR Language I.* Chicago: SRA/McGraw-Hill.

Foorman, B.R., Francis, D.J., Fletcher, J.M., Schatschneider, C., & Mehta, P. (1998). The role of instruction in learning to read: Preventing reading failure in at-risk children. *Journal of Educational Psychology. 90*, 37-55.

Olson, R. (1998). *Report of the National Research Council on Early Reading: Implications for practice.* Presented at the Urban Symposium on Literacy, Los Angeles, CA, April.

Open Court Reading (1995). *Collections for Young Scholars.* Peru, IL: SRA/McGraw-Hill.

Slavin, R. E., & Madden, N. (1989). What works for students at risk: A research synthesis. *Educational Leadership, 64*, 4-13.

Snow, C.E., Burns, M.S. & Griffin, P. (1998). *Preventing reading difficulties in young children.* Washington, DC: National Academy Press.

Stahl, S.A., Osborn, J., Lehr, F. (1990). A summary of: *Beginning to read: Thinking and learning about print.* Urbana-Champaign, ILL: Center for the Study of Reading.

Standardized Test of Assessment for Reading (1995). Wisconsin Rapids, WI: Advantage Learning Systems, Inc.

Torgesen, J.K. & Bryant, B. (1994). *Test of Phonological Awareness.* Austin, TX: Pro-Ed Publishers, Inc.

Waterford Institute (1995). *Waterford Early Reading Program, Level I.* Menlo Park, CA: Electronic Education, Inc.

Woodcock, R.W., & Johnson, M. B. (1989). *Woodcock-Johnson Psycho-Educational Battery-Revised.* Allen, TX: DLM/Teaching Resources

Figure Caption

Figure 1: Changes in year end reading performance of children during period of rapid curriculum changes in reading

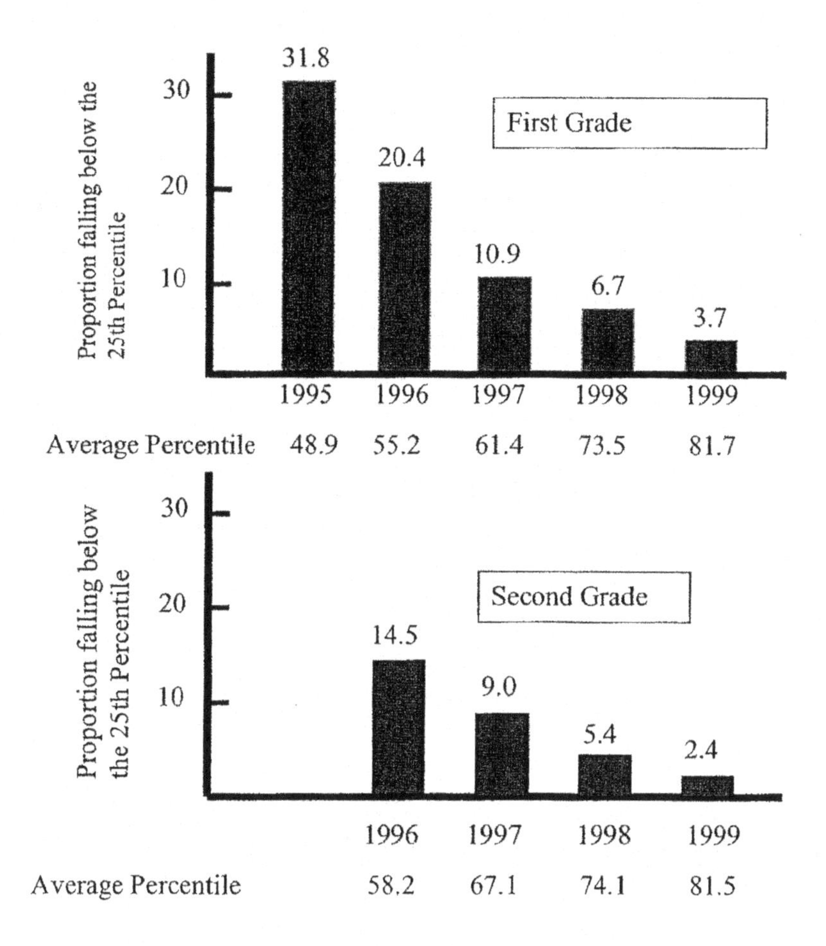

APPENDIX F - WRITTEN STATEMENT OF JOSEPH F. KOVALESKI, DIRECTOR OF PUPIL SERVICES, CORNWALL-LEBANON SCHOOL DISTRICT, LITITZ, PENNSYLVANIA

TESTIMONY PRESENTED TO THE U.S. HOUSE OF REPRESENTATIVES SUBCOMMITTEE ON EDUCATION REFORM AT THE HEARING ON "LEARNING DISABILITIES AND EARLY INTERVENTION STRATEGIES: HOW TO REFORM THE SPECIAL EDUCATION REFERRAL AND IDENTIFICATION PROCESS"

Presented by:
Joseph F. Kovaleski, D.Ed.
Cornwall-Lebanon (PA) School District

June 6, 2002

My name is Joseph Kovaleski. I am the Director of Pupil Services for the Cornwall-Lebanon School District in Lebanon, PA. Professionally, I am a nationally certified school psychologist and a member of the National Association of School Psychologists. I have directed special education and pupil services for school districts and regional education agencies since 1977.

The issue that we are addressing today, the reform of the special education referral and identification process, has been a controversial and important one since I entered the field of special education 25 years ago. We have long understood that too many students have been over-identified as having learning disabilities. We have seen limited funds for special education overwhelmed by too many students in the system. As students have been found eligible for special education, we have seen general education come to an understanding that it has little responsibility for students with even transient academic and behavior problems. Many teachers have come to believe that any student with any difficulty may have hidden disabilities that prevent them from succeeding in the regular classroom.

Thankfully, during the last decade, we in Pennsylvania had an opportunity to reverse this trend. Today I would like to testify to the success we have had with early intervention with elementary students using prereferral interventions. From 1990 to 1997, I served as the state director of the Instructional Support Team (IST) project in Pennsylvania. This project succeeded in implementing instructional support teams in over 1,700 schools in 500 school districts. I have also consulted with school districts in a number of other states on initiating the IST program in those areas. In my work with prereferral teams, I have also been in contact with other researchers and practitioners who have had equal success with similar models in other states.

In Pennsylvania, we have had very positive results in limiting over-identification and providing tangible support to general education teachers with our instructional support team model. The process utilizes building-based teams to precisely assess students with academic and behavioral difficulties through curriculum-based assessment and other procedures. The team provides in-class support to the regular classroom teacher over a 50-day period to determine whether the application of effective instructional procedures changes the rate of learning for the student. Students who display meaningful gains through ongoing monitoring of their performance are not referred for a full and individual evaluation for special education. Those students who display resistance to these interventions are referred for evaluation, and typically are later identified as needing special education. These prereferral procedures are, in my view, the most effective way of determining whether a student's difficulties are the result of a lack of instruction rather than a disability, a provision which I was very gratified to see included in the 1997 IDEA amendments.

When schools in Pennsylvania implemented ISTs, 85% of the students identified for the process did not need a further full and individual evaluation for special education. Schools that implemented ISTs had their rates of identification of students with disabilities either plateau or, in many cases, decrease. In a published study on the results of this program, we found that students undergoing the IST process displayed improved achievement on academic learning time measures when schools implemented the program at a high degree of fidelity.

From this experience in Pennsylvania, as well as from my interactions with colleagues from across the country, I offer the following conclusions:

<u>Referrals for special education eligibility screening can be greatly reduced by using an effective prereferral intervention model.</u>

Our experiences with ISTs in Pennsylvania have been replicated frequently with similar models such as instructional consultation teams, problem solving teams, Project ACHIEVE and other models throughout the country. In both published studies of these models as well as reports from practitioners, we know that there is a large group of students who can learn if supported interventions are delivered before pervasive learning problems and learned helplessness develop. Some of these students display rapid growth in their learning rates when provided with effective instruction. Others may continue to need support throughout their school career, but nonetheless can be effectively educated in a general education setting without special education.

<u>The testing process itself, as it is typically implemented, leads to over-identification.</u>

Without a procedure for early intervention, schools typically rely on the so-called "refer-test-place" practice. It is well known that testing itself, without early intervention, often leads to three types of placement errors. First, students who are academically deficient and resistant to good instruction may still not qualify for special education services because they lack a discrepancy from their assessed intelligent quotients. These students are often identified as slow learners, and in essence are expected to fail. The second error occurs when students with higher IQs with marginal problems are identified for special education because their academic achievement is discrepant from their intelligence, even if these deficiencies could be addressed adequately in the general education program. Finally, testing as the sole identification procedure may result in disproportionate representation of minority students and English language learners in special education programs. Many school personnel will report that not only are there too many students being identified as learning disabled, but the wrong students are qualifying for these programs.

<u>The best way to identify the right students as eligible for special education is by appraising their response to effective instruction.</u>

There is now a 20-year history of research and practice in methods that would allow schools to identify students as eligible for special education through an evaluation of their response to effective instruction. Through methods such as curriculum-based measurement, schools can assess students' rate of learning while they are being provided with strategies that are research-based and supported by instructional support teams. These measurement procedures not only guide the intervention process in a search for what will work for the student, but also produce a reliable and valid set of data that can be used in the eligibility process. With these methods, we can identify students who are not only discrepant from grade expectations, but also those who show resistance to instruction even when carefully taught.

There needs to be a fully funded early literacy program that provides intensive intervention for students who are at risk for not learning to read by the third grade.

The current identification process leading to identification of learning disabilities and other disabling conditions has been correctly criticized because needed special education programs are not delivered until students are discrepant enough from their expected levels, typically in third grade or beyond. By that time, the window for establishing early literacy is passed, and it becomes increasingly difficult to bring students to expected levels of achievement. It is difficult to identity which of the students entering elementary school who show signs they will have difficulty learning to read will ultimately be classifiable as learning disabled. We can, however, identify which students are in need of intensive and timely early literacy programs, and we are very heartened by recent research that shows that these interventions (e.g., phonological and phonemic awareness training) have impressive results with children. These students should not be identified as eligible for special education to receive needed services. Rather, school districts should be allowed to utilize special education funds for early interventions in a non-categorical format, as a method to determine who will ultimately need long-term special education services.

There needs to be coordination at the federal, state, and local levels among federal programs that address overlapping issues such as the development of literacy.

It matters little to school districts which funding stream is utilized to provide needed early intervention. For most school districts, administrators try to patch together federal, state and local funds to provide needed programs. However, with different funding streams, different and often competing mandates result in fragmented educational programs that do not articulate well with each other. It is not unusual to find persons with jobs titles such as special education teacher, remedial reading teacher, and remedial math teacher all working in uncoordinated ways in the same school, while large numbers of students continue to fail to meet basic competencies. There needs to be clear directions to school personnel that services should be coordinated so that a seamless system that prevents students from "falling between the cracks" can be developed. Again, under the direction of the building principal, instructional support teams can be especially useful in assuring that the continuum of services works for children.

Teachers, administrators, and related services personnel address students' needs best when they work together in prereferral teams like instructional support teams.

As schools endeavor to provide services so that all children receive effective educational programs, coordination through a core team, like an instructional support team, is extremely beneficial. Not only can such teams provide assistance to teachers in dealing with individual students who require special interventions, they can also monitor which students are falling behind or are developing problems, so that services can be coordinated so students get the help they need when they need it. Recently developed procedures such as data mining can be especially useful in the hands of building-based teams.

The preamble to the 1997 amendments of IDEA articulated the problems with the over-identification of students as eligible for special education and identified prereferral intervention as an effective technique for assuring that only students who have verifiable disabilities are provided with special education. Unfortunately, in spite of this assertion in the preamble, there was no language in the law itself that stipulated a formal prereferral process. It is time to consider specific language that directs the development of these teams in all schools.

The screening and early identification process needs to address students' emotional and behavioral needs as well as their academic needs.

Much of the focus of this discussion has been on early literacy and the attendant problems of identification of learning disabilities. However, as a school psychologist, I am well aware that a large number of students being identified as needing special education have emotional and behavioral difficulties that lead to both learning and adjustment problems in school. The screening and evaluation process needs to emphasize procedures and interventions for behavioral as well as academic difficulties. The National Academy of Sciences report on minority students in special and gifted education found that the second most common reason for referrals to special education is school behavior. As such, an equal amount of attention should be placed on interventions that have proven to address behavioral issues and mitigate discipline problems. We will need to provide teachers and other school staff with the necessary professional development to address these behaviors through positive behavioral supports.

In summary, we have argued many of the issues raised today for decades. We are now at a point where research has caught up with rhetoric. I believe that the recommendations that I have made would increase the effectiveness of the general education program which provides services for at-risk students, would facilitate the prevention of academic and behavioral difficulties at primary and intermediate grades, and would reserve needed special education services for those students who are truly eligible.

Thank you for this opportunity to address this forum.

Joseph F. Kovaleski, D.Ed.
Director of Pupil Services
Cornwall-Lebanon School District
105 E. Evergreen Road
Lebanon, PA 17042
717/272-2031 (office)
717/274-2786 (fax)
Email (office): jkovaleski@clsd.k12.pa.us

Publications about IST

Brainstorming helps educators address concerns. (1996). Inclusive Education Programs, 3, 1, 11-12.

Conway, S. J., & Kovaleski, J. F. (1998). A model for statewide special education reform: Pennsylvania's instructional support teams. International Journal of Educational Reform, 7(4), Oct. 1998, 1-7.

Hartman, W. T. & Fay, T. A. (1996). Cost-effectiveness of instructional support teams in Pennsylvania. Journal of Education Finance, 21, 555-580.

Kovaleski, J.F. (in press). Best practices in implementing pre-referral intervention teams. In A. Thomas and J. Grimes (eds.), Best practices in school psychology IV. Washington, DC: National Association of School Psychologists.

Kovaleski, J. F., Gickling, E. E., Morrow, H., & Swank, P. (1999). High versus low implementation of instructional support teams: A case for maintaining program fidelity. Remedial ar Special Education, 20, 170-183.

Kovaleski, J. F., Tucker, J. A., & Duffy, D. J. (1995). School reform through instructional support: The Pennsylvania initiative (Part I). NASP Communiqué, 23, 8 (insert).

Kovaleski, J. F., Lowery, P. E., & Gickling, E. E. (1995). School reform through instructional support - The instructional evaluation: The Pennsylvania initiative (Part 2). NASP Communiqué, 23, 14, 16-17.

Kovaleski, J. F., Tucker, J. A., & Stevens, L. (1996). Bridging special and regular education: The Pennsylvania initiative. Educational Leadership, 53, 44-47.

Publications about Prereferral Intervention

Batsche, G.M. & Knoff, H.M. (1995). Project AHIEVE: Analyzing a school reform process for at-risk and underachieving students. School Psychology Review, 24, 579-603.

Carter, J., & Sugai, G. (1989). Survey of prereferral practices: Responses from state departments of education. Exceptional Children, 55, 298-302.

Chalfant, J.C. & Pysh, M.V. (1989). Teacher assistance teams: Five descriptive studies on 96 teams. Remedial and Special Education, 10, 49-58.

Flugum, K. & Reschly, K. (1994). Prereferral interventions: Quality indices and outcomes. Journal of School Psychology, 32(1), 1-14.

Fuchs, D., Fuchs, L.S., & Bahr, M. W. (1990). Mainstream assistance teams: A scientific basis for the art of consultation. Exceptional Children, 57, 128-139.

Fuchs, D., Fuchs, L.S., Bahr, M.W., Fernstrom, P. & Stecker, P.M. (1990). Prereferral intervention: A prescriptive approach. Exceptional Children, 56, 493-513.

Graden, J. L., Casey, A., and Bonstrom, O. (1985). Implementing a prereferral intervention system: Part II. The data. Exceptional Children, 51: 487-486.

Graden, J.L., Casey, A., & Christenson, S.L. (1985). Implementing a prereferral intervention system: Part I. The model. Exceptional Children, 51, 377-384.

Nelson, J.R., Smith, D.J., Taylor, L., Dodd, J.M., & Reavis, K. (1991). Prereferral interventions: A review of the research. Education and Treatment of Children, 14(3), 243-253.

Rosenfield, S. (1987). Instructional consultation. Hillsdale, NJ: Lawrence Erlbaum Associates, Inc.

Rosenfield, S. & Gravois, T. (1996). Instructional consultation teams: Collaborating for cha New York: Guilford.

Safran, S. P. & Safran, J.S. (1996). Intervention assistance programs and prereferral te: Directions for the twenty-first century. Remedial and Special Education, 17, 363-369.

Schrag, J.A. & Henderson, K. (1996). School-based intervention assistance teams and impact on special education. Alexandria, VA: National Association of State Directors of Sp Education.

Sindelar, P.T., Griffin, C.C., Smith, S.W. & Watanabe, A.K. (1992). Prereferral intervention: Encouraging notes on preliminary findings. The Elementary School Journal, 20, 388-408.

APPENDIX G - WRITTEN STATEMENT OF DAVID W. GORDON, SUPERINTENDENT, ELK GROVE UNIFIED SCHOOL DISTRICT, ELK GROVE, CALIFORNIA

Elk Grove Unified School District's Model of Student Failure Prevention and Intervention

Neverstreaming

Learning Disabilities and Early Intervention Strategies: How to Reform the Special Education Referral and Identification Process

June 6, 2002
Washington, D.C.

Presented by: David W. Gordon
Superintendent
Elk Grove Unified School District
Elk Grove, California

Neverstreaming: Never allowing a child to leave the advantage of the mainstream in the first place.

Elk Grove Unified School District's Model of Student Failure Prevention and Intervention

Neverstreaming: The Birth of a Vision

Neverstreaming literally means as its title implies, never allowing a child to leave the advantage of the mainstream in the first place. The process leading to the Neverstreaming plan resulted from years of students having no other option. It was either make it in the general education classroom or be referred for special education. Now, there is a system that works. Neverstreaming provides a process for preventing students from reaching a point of failure in which they would become "lifers in a special education world."

Neverstreaming was born out of the anticipation of a new beginning. This new beginning emerged as a result of continual frustration and spiraling placements in special education classes on the basis of learning disabilities. As the district's population grew and the diversity of students changed over time, more and more students were finding their way into learning disability programs. More students were placed in this program as they aged through the primary grades. Students ended up in special education at a time when reading was the most dependent variable of their academic success. Pupils between the ages of eight and eleven represented the highest portion of students identified with learning disabilities in our school district.

Directly related to the aspect of learning to read is the importance of reading fluently and with comprehension skills while moving to intermediate elementary school grades and then into the secondary school levels. As a result, many of our educational approaches were driven by the spiraling reading demands of the curriculum. Teachers responsible for educating these students were finding themselves in a highly frustrated and ambiguous situation. They could not depend on the students reading their own texts because they didn't know how to incorporate reading into the curriculum. As a result, an interdisciplinary committee of various professionals began to explore the situation and analyze data to terminate causes of the situation.

Today the number of students requiring special education has been cut from 16% to 8.4% respectively by providing prevention services. The reduction in special education from 1992 to present was not the result of denying students access to badly needed alternative services but through providing curriculum and instructional methods in a coordinated fashion that changed the service delivery systems for student interventions.

Neverstreaming reduces the need for students to be taken from the mainstream for long periods of time in order to receive assistance. Historically, special education has a record of removing students from the mainstream of education but conversely it has a very poor record of returning students to the mainstream over the long term. Directly related is the eligibility criteria used to identify children thought to have a learning disability. The significant discrepancy model demands a discrepancy between achievement and cognition to such a significant degree that it theoretically interferes with the child's learning and thus indicates a referral for special education. This eligibility criterion causes a dilemma because children must demonstrate a significant degree of failure prior to reaching the eligibility standard under law.

Along the way to reaching special education eligibility, typically little is done in terms of intensive interventions to prevent the inevitability of special education referral. Neverstreaming does not use criteria that is based on achievement comparison to cognition, but focuses on diagnostic and prescriptive teaching in reading.

The vast majority of children identified for special education nationally are labeled as learning disabled. Through a review of many earlier Individual Education Programs, it was found in our district that 80% of the students in special education with learning disabilities had a basis for eligibility in reading. What is known about reading disabilities now per the studies done by the National Institutes of Children's Health and Development and others is that the significant discrepancy model is incidental to the actual reading problems of the child and the ability to learn reading. Commonly we depend on the discrepancy model to denote failure in reading significant enough to qualify for help through special education.

Neverstreaming changes the paradigm from failing first to preventing failure in the first place. By changing that paradigm through constant vigilance, we actually promote prevention over reactive models. Prevention means that you prevent the child from backsliding educationally to the point where support is only available through separate program models that require long-term remediation with very little chance of catching up to the grade level group.

The Matthew effect, which has been cited specifically by reading experts in the field indicates that when it comes to reading, the rich do get richer and the poor get poorer as seen in the reading abilities necessary to move from elementary to middle to high school reading success. The extension of reading prowess is a prerequisite to secondary curriculum and depends on a rich vocabulary, increasing use of complex syntactical structure, and strong comprehension of expository text.

Neverstreaming prevents children from failing first by becoming proficient readers and obtaining academic success. Standards and evaluation data indicate that Neverstreaming does produce exceptional results.

Neverstreaming's existence has been celebrated through numerous recognitions and awards. The most significant of which was the 1997 prestigious Golden Bell Award granted by the CA School Boards Association. Neverstreaming programs have been visited by over 500 school districts, including New York City Schools, districts from Ohio, Wyoming, Arizona, Colorado, and Nevada. The Elk Grove Model of Intervention/Prevention Planning and Service Delivery is good for kids because it doesn't leave children behind.

LEAVING NO CHILD BEHIND

Search and Serve procedures provide the logical process for early identification of students at risk of academic failure at the school or preschool level. Child development research indicates that the earlier a student's learning problems are discovered, the higher likelihood proper remediation can improve school success. Having a strong Child Find process will assist with student success in early grades. It is clear that with early identification and intervention, academic subjects such as reading can be greatly enhanced. "Failing to leave the third grade with adequate reading levels assures a 74% chance that reading problems will persist through the 9th grade or higher." (NICHD Reid Lyon)

EARLY INTERVENTION/PREVENTION

Typical intervention programs that lead to special education identification rely on the student first demonstrating a degree of failure before any significant assistance is obtained. Traditional school approaches often result in the student's failure persisting until a point of eligibility is reached through the discrepancy model for specific learning disabilities.

The "discrepancy model" describes the eligibility criteria used to qualify a student with a specific learning disability (SLD). Because SLD is not scientifically identified by neuro/physiological evidence developed medically, it is based on a theoretical comparison of student achievement compared to cognitive ability. To prove the child has a SLD, there must be a discrepancy between the student's assessed cognitive level and his/her achievement level. For example, a student tested within the normal range of intellectual functioning, but whose achievement is significantly below grade level, may be experiencing a learning disability that is preventing the child from performing at his or her intellectual potential. However, to reach a point-spread difference broad enough for eligibility to occur may take several years of academic failure. Earlier intervention may have remediated the learning gaps of the student and prevented grade level delays.

When the comparison between ability and achievement finally results in a point deficit high enough for students to reach eligibility, placements are then made to the resource specialist or special day class special education programs. Typical practice across most states results in few schools making successful interventions prior to the student's continued failure and eventual referral for special education assessment. This is evidenced by the exceedingly high number of learning-disabled students placed in self-contained programs for the majority of the school day.

This fail-first phenomenon has been confirmed by reviewing eligibility data that shows the actual time frame when most students become identified as learning disabled. Usually students between the ages of 8 and 11 years old are at the highest risk of identification. By such time in their school careers, deficits in reading and other academic subjects usually have reached a point of frustration and significant delay when compared to their grade level expectancies. Proper academic interventions may, in fact, prevent the need for them to receive more restrictive services, which all too often result in life long schooling in a parallel education system.

A parallel system occurs as a result of students so far from grade level expectancies that they are never able to catch up to their grade level peers. Students who are in special day classes with learning disabilities have little chance of moving to their grade level classrooms in general education. As the core subjects become more challenging at each progressive grade level, year to year academic growth is not good enough for the special day class (SDC) based students to move to the core curriculum in the least restrictive environment. Most of these students start out in special day classes two or more years academically behind their peers and usually this gap broadens from grade to grade. There is an insufficient systemic process defined that requires states to apply prevention/intervention strategies that could break the cycle of special education placements and student failure in the general education classroom.

Pre-Referral Prevention/Intervention
Federal law, under IDEA 97, requires that students receive the benefit of supplemental aids and services prior to referring them for special education assessment. Intervention and prevention services are legally required to prevent other factors from being incorrectly identified as learning disabilities. These include educational disadvantages, cultural differences, primary languages other than English, sensory deficits from vision or hearing impairments, and lack of consistent school attendance. Each of these factors may mimic achievement and behavior problems of the students with SLD. However, the causes in these cases cannot be attributable to a disability.

To prevent false positive referrals for special education services, the state and federal laws pertaining to specific learning disabilities must be more specifically aligned. School districts need to incorporate systems that address student academic problems long before special education assessment is requested. Interventions must be documented to demonstrate that considerations for the student's learning needs were heroically addressed before referral.

Teachers play a critical role in providing support to the implementation of pre-referral services delivered at the local school level. An intervention/prevention collaborative model permits students to be served based on need, rather than based on special education identification. Pre-referral interventions allow teachers to spend most of their time teaching rather than testing. Schools may tailor the intervention programs to students' needs. Each program must use diagnostic teaching techniques and an accelerated learning pace, driven by individual student data that aids the teacher in informing instruction.

Students who achieve on the fringe of development levels may be students who encounter academic and pre-academic problems. Learning deficits may hinder the child's ability to learn to read which is the most important part of primary grade education and preparation for later success in school.

Data Based Decision Making
Student data collection is essential. A student data collection process used in elementary and secondary schools allows teachers to interpret and record data. Individual student performance defines the remediation strategies needed. This data should be collected through a routine cycle that is part of the school's academic improvement process.

Specific academic information is necessary in order to provide appropriate and effective intervention planning along with the student's general attendance, health, academic history, and recent standardized test data. This information provides baseline performance indicators from which instructional strategies, settings, and intensity of the interventions can be determined. Routine data collection and analysis forces a tighter curriculum alignment and monitoring of student progress in reading, math, and written and expressive/receptive language development, particularly for English language learners.

The teachers review student progress throughout the year. It is reviewed in an organized data rich process at recurring school team conferences. Teams may vary in design; however, multi-disciplinary expertise results in working together for common solutions. The analysis of student data and other pertinent information is the basis for prescribing appropriate student interventions. School team members analyze the data and then determine appropriate services for the student or family.

The analysis of performance data and its effects on student need is the driving force of the intervention levels. Data is used to set student and program goals through a collaborative and strategically coordinated plan in which the classroom teacher plays a principal role. Databased decision-making fuels the pre-referral interventions for each child to succeed, avoid retention, and remain in the least restrictive environment.

Diagnostic Teaching and Intervention

Services must be flexibly designed to target specific needs and monitor progress toward student goals. Goals are revised and instruction modified to match the changing needs and progress of students, thus avoiding the lockstep process of tracking. Services are fluid and the student's rate of improved performance drives the intervention levels.

The multidisciplinary team provides a structure whereby teachers, administrators, and specialists review student body academic progress. Appropriate modifications or services are determined and assigned as student needs first arise. Through this structure, student needs can be addressed early in a student's school career.

By accelerating the learning curve of the student with an intensive program, the student receives one to three hours of instruction in the affected area per day. In this way, the student could receive small group instruction, one-to-one tutoring or differentiated instruction from the regular education teacher in consult with a reading specialist or special educator. At least an 8-12 week intervention period is key to determining whether the diagnostic interventions will have an effect on accelerating the student's learning levels in academic achievement. For example, a teacher utilizing various Curriculum Based Measures regarding words per minute in reading would expect to see approximately a six-month growth rate in 8-12 weeks. Without criterion-referenced measures or individual testing, teachers would not be able to determine when the intervention process should be abandoned and/or a referral made to a Student Assessment Team.

The Benchmark Level

These students may be able to meet the minimum standard requirements at each grade level, however, they may require some additional support in order to keep from falling behind. These students can generally meet minimum requirements, but admission to a four-year college would be difficult Re-teaching, study groups, parent help at home, and additional practice are usually helpful. Students at this level of intervention can generally be successful in a general education classroom without specialized support.

Specific diagnostic teaching by the classroom teacher, utilizing re-teaching skills, and frequent checks for understanding, help these students become successful. Flexible and varied grouping strategies that offer different pacing within the classroom should be used to assist students with expressive/receptive language tasks.

- The benchmark level of intervention is designed for students that have minor deficits in certain content areas. Students requiring this level of support usually score between the 23rd and 39th percentile on the SAT9 and fall in the 4th stanine. This level of performance is considered low average. Approximately 17 percent of students nationwide score in the 4th stanine. These students can generally meet minimum requirements, but admission to a four-year college would be difficult. Students at this level of intervention can generally be successful in a general education classroom without specialized support.

Cooperative Conference - Benchmark Level

Cooperative Conference Team Members
Classroom Teacher, Specialists, Support Staff, Administrator,
Teacher reviews progress towards standards and benchmarks for all students' needs based on data matrix. Team reviews all students' intervention needs.

General education and support services collaborate to meet the individual needs of all students by making the necessary modifications in the mainstream classroom to ensure success for all.

The Core Curriculum is supported through scaffolding of instruction and collaborative teaching.

Benchmark Intervention		
Characteristics	**Appropriate Interventions**	**Suggested Materials and Programs**
Generally good progress – may encounter temporary or minor difficulties.	Group flexibly to pre-teach or re-teach specific skills. Scaffold students to	Intervention materials provided with core curriculum, including the "Take-Home" books

Needs not critical, but require attention to prevent more serious difficulties.	assure success during regular instruction. Provide practice that reinforces targeted skills.	Scaffolding strategies Group for multi-syllabic decoding

Case Study
Phan is a seventh grade student attending middle school. She was an ELL student, but no longer requires ELL support. Phan's teachers note that she is a very hard working student, but seems to have difficulty with some reading tasks. Vocabulary concepts seem to be difficult for Phan. These deficits in vocabulary seem to keep Phan from reaching her full potential as a student. Phan's SAT9 scores generally fall between the 23rd and 39th percentile or the 4th stanine. Phan's SAT9 profile follows:

Subtest and Totals	No. of Items	Raw Score	Scaled Score	National PR-S	National NCE
Total Reading	84	46	717	25-4	36.0
Vocabulary	30	11	621	17-3	26.0
Comprehension	54	32	756	26-4	37.0
Mathematics	48	20	700	37-4	42.0
Language	48	12	663	31-4	39.0
Lang. Mechanics	24	12	664	33-4	40.7
Lang. Expression	24	14	663	33-4	39.6
Science	40	17	672	36-4	42.5
Social Studies	40	14	645	27-4	37.1

Phan's Content Clusters show a deficit in the area of reading vocabulary. This deficit seems to keep Phan in the low average range of achievement. The deficit in vocabulary also is reflected in other content areas requiring vocabulary skills.

Phan's language-arts teachers, using this data, design a small-group direct instruction component for Phan to focus on vocabulary development. Support curriculum is supplementary to the core curriculum for Phan. Peer tutors are also assigned for Phan to assist with vocabulary development. Phan's teacher will continue to assess and modify the supplementary curriculum to ensure it's effectiveness in developing stronger vocabulary skills, thus providing Phan with the opportunity to develop her full potential, while fully participating in the general education core curriculum.

The Strategic Level
The strategic level of intervention is designed for students that have several deficits in certain content areas. Students requiring specific intervention typically score between the 11th and 22nd percentile on the SAT9 and fall in the 3rd stanine. Approximately 12% of the students nationwide fall within these parameters. Students scoring at this level require a modified curriculum focusing on the areas of deficit. These students can generally be served in the general education classroom with specialized support

through an intervention program. These interventions are necessary to prevent further deficits in communication skills that could lead to eventual referral for special education.

Strategic Level Interventions in the General Education Classroom
Students at the Strategic Level will require specific interventions in the general education classroom.

Strategic Intervention		
Characteristics	**Appropriate Interventions**	**Suggested Materials and Programs**
One or two standard deviations below the mean on standardized assessments. Require systematic and occasionally intensive support.	Group for more intensive support from teacher. Provide extended day or twilight instruction. Adjust schedule for additional language arts during day.	Multi-syllabic decoding or similar program Fluency Scaffold comprehension Modify class assignments A Language intervention program

The student is in danger of failing to meet one or more minimum standard requirements for grade level expectancies. These students will need to be taught elements in prerequisite skill areas of speech and language development necessary for educational success particularly in reading and written language skills. They also require more intensive reinforced instruction from the specialist.

The students requiring specific interventions will need modified instruction and consideration for learning modalities, memory techniques, and opportunities to practice what has been learned.
Data from the Co-Op meeting will be required to identify specific deficits to be targeted for direct instruction. Specialists may possibly come into the class in order to provide the necessary instructional strategies. This student has the potential to make effective progress but needs a support system from identified staff in the classroom. The students requiring strategic interventions will need modified instruction and consideration for learning modalities, memory techniques, and opportunities to practice what has been learned.

For example, support curriculum including leveled readers may be needed to address the student's specific needs in vocabulary, while receiving a modified core curriculum. An extended day program as well as summer school may be needed to focus on identified deficits in order to avoid the possibility of retention. Ongoing assessment will be required to monitor student progress.

Case Study
Sally is a ninth grade student attending high school. She has never been retained, but has required additional instruction in the form of intersession to graduate from middle school. Sally's teacher noted in her cum file that she has difficulty with reading comprehension and it is affecting her performance in language-arts, history and science. They also noted that she is discouraged with school and her attendance and behavior suffered. Sally's standardized test scores generally fall between the 11th and

22nd percentile or well below average. Without specific reading support from a language intervention program, Sally's prospect of meeting minimal graduation standards is suspect. Following is Sally's SAT9 profile:

Subtest and Totals	No. of Items	Raw Score	Scaled Score	National PR-S	National NCE
Total Reading	84	43	669	15-3	28.0
Vocabulary	30	18	690	35-4	40.0
Comprehension	54	24	655	13-3	25.0
Mathematics	48	19	688	36-4	42.5
Language	48	22	636	22-3	33.0
Lang. Mechanics	24	11	631	29-4	35.0
Lang. Expression	24	12	602	24-3	31.0
Science	40	10	543	20-3	23.0
Social Studies	40	9	489	22-3	25.0

Sally's Content Clusters show major deficits in reading comprehension, scoring well below grade level expectancy in the following reading areas: functional, critical analysis, interpretation and initial understanding. Content area reading such as that required in social studies and science is directly linked to these deficits in Sally's performance.

Sally's teachers, using this data, decide that Sally will require a language program intervention taught by a trained teacher with the support of the specialist. Sally will receive direct instruction in a classroom setting to address these deficits. While receiving a modified core curriculum, support curriculum including leveled readers will be provided by the teachers to address Sally's specific needs in vocabulary. Sally's science and history teachers will also receive modified curriculum focusing on the identified deficits. Sally is also recommended to attend an extended day program as well as summer school. The curriculum for summer school and extended day will focus on her identified deficits in order to avoid the possibility of retention or special education. Ongoing assessment will be required to monitor Sally's progress.

Intensive Interventions

The intensive level of intervention is designed for students severely delayed in their academic performance. Students requiring this level of intervention typically score at/or below the 10th percentile on the SAT9 and fall in the 1st and 2nd stanine. Approximately 11% of the students nationwide fall within these parameters. Without drastic interventions these students are in danger of school failure and possibly going through life functionally illiterate.

These interventions may occur in a learning center, resource setting, or reading lab that measures progress toward student goals. Identified students will require interventions outside the general education classroom. Small group instruction with support from specialists at the school site will be necessary.

When interventions do not show improvement in the student, a Student Success Team may consider possible special education assessment. However, the purpose is to intervene early, thus avoiding failure in the long term. The goal is to return the student

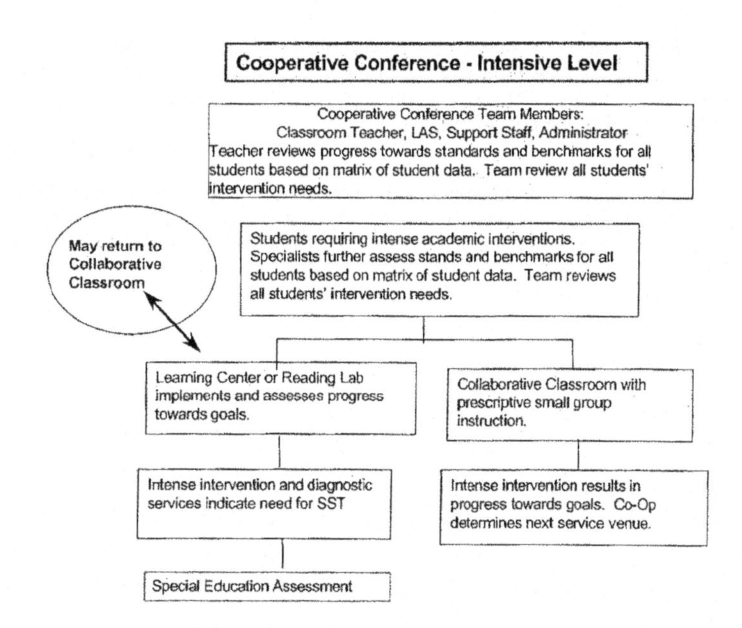

to the general education classroom where assistance and services in the least restrictive environment are continued.

The graphic above depicts the interventions for the Intensive Level. General education teachers receive assistance from the support specialist to prescribe those interventions necessary to enhance identified academic weaknesses.

Intensive Intervention		
Characteristics	**Appropriate Interventions**	**Suggested Materials and Programs**
Seriously at risk because of chronically low performance on multiple measures. Performs well below the mean.	Refer to Cooperative Conference for discussion and development of plan. Similar to strategic, but more severe difficulties.	*Open Court* *Breaking the Code* *Language!*

The Cooperative Conference Team decides which interventions are needed outside the general education classroom. The general education teacher implements instructional strategies through small group instruction with support from specialists. If the intervention cycle is successful, the student returns to a collaborative classroom (Strategic Level). When interventions do not show improvement in the student, a

Student Study Team may consider possible special education assessment. The purpose is to intervene early thus avoiding failure in the long term. The goal is to return the student to the Strategic Level of support where assistance and services in the least restrictive environment are continued.

Case Study
Johnny is an eighth grade student attending middle school. Johnny was retained in the 1st grade, with a notation in his cum folder sighting poor academic performance and immaturity. During the next 6 years, Johnny's educational performance was noted as slow learner, possible special education (didn't qualify), high rate of transience, poor attendance, increased inappropriate behaviors, and social promotion. Johnny's standardized test scores were consistently below the 10th percentile and he was labeled as being functionally illiterate. High school graduation was very unlikely. Following is Johnny's SAT9 scores from his 7th grade assessment:

Subtest and Totals	No. of Items	Raw Score	Scaled Score	National PR-S	National NCE
Total Reading	84	22	402	9-2	14.2
Vocabulary	30	10	351	7-2	12.0
Comprehension	54	12	423	8-2	13.3
Mathematics	48	12	507	15-3	26.6
Language	48	20	433	10-2	16.1
Lang. Mechanics	24	9	401	9-2	16.0
Lang. Expression	24	11	345	8-2	15.1
Science	40	15	289	7-2	14.1
Social Studies	40	12	301	6-2	13.1

Johnny's Content Clusters show him scoring below average in all areas comprising his total reading and total math. Science and Social Studies seem to reflect his difficulty with reading. Johnny's teachers administer several informal assessments that profile him as extremely deficient in basic phoneme awareness, decoding and reading at approximately 46 words per minute. Johnny's comprehension is at approximately the 3rd grade level, reflecting his inability to decode and read fluently.

His teachers receive assistance from the speech and language specialist to prescribe those interventions necessary to enhance phonemic awareness, phonics and expressive/receptive language. Using the data, they decide that Johnny requires an extremely structured reading intervention program. The intervention program placement test places Johnny at the lowest level of intervention. Johnny's intense reading and language needs require him to receive a minimum of 90 minutes per day of the direct instruction in this program, (Block Schedule: one 90 minute block per day per year, Regular Schedule: two periods per day per year) supplemented with additional time in either extended day or intersession. A two to three year plan of intervention is designed to help Johnny get back on track in reading, expressive/receptive language, social studies and science.

The specialist works with students like Johnny over a short term. During the intervention period, the classroom teacher provides interventions along with the specialist staff. Data results, which are routinely taken during the intervention period, indicate those students that did not make substantial gains. Following an 8-12 week period of intervention, these students are referred to the Student Success Team and possible special education assessment

Intervention Service Delivery Flow Chart

The chart below represents the flow of intervention service delivery for students at risk of retention and or special education assessment. This flow chart demonstrates the levels of intervention and the application of these services by group and highlights the process taken from the Cooperative Conference through the establishment of the services by intervention level.

Cooperative Conference Chart of Interventions

Cooperative Conference Team Members

Classroom Teacher,Specialist, Categorical Staff, Administrator, Support Staff

Action:

•Classroom teacher reviews data matrix of students regarding their progress towards standards and benchmarks.

•Team designs immediate interventions for identified students

Benchmark Group

Characteristics:

Generally good progress may have temporary or minor difficulties. Needs require attention to prevent more serious difficulties

Remains in general education classroom

Interventions:

•Group flexibly to pre-teach or re-teach specific skills.

•Scaffold students to assure success during regular instruction

•provide practice that reinforces targeted skills

•Small group direct instruction

•Group for multi-syllabic decoding

•On-going Assessment to determine further need

Strategic Group

Characteristics:

One or two standard deviations below the mean on standardized assessments. Require systematic and occasionally intensive support

Interventions:

•Generally served in the regular classroom with specialized support focusing on areas of deficit.

•Group for more intensive support from teacher.

•Provide extended day instruction

•Adjust schedule for additional language arts during day.

•Multi-syllabic decoding or similar program

•Fluency

•Scaffold comprehension

•Modify class assignments

•On-going assessment to determine further need.

Intensive Group

Characteristics: Seriously at risk because of chronically low performance on multiple measures. Performs well below the mean.

Interventions:

•Highly structured intervention program

•supplemented with extended day or intersession

•Two-to-three year plan of intervention designed to track reading, language, science and social studies

•On-going assessment to determine progress and further interventions

David W. Gordon
Subcommittee on Education Reform
Washington, D.C., June 6, 2002

INTERVENTION/PREVENTION PLANNING AND SERVICES

IDEA 97 supports early intervention/prevention planning and services as an effort to prevent both long-term special education and parallel systems that are far removed from the district's core curriculum. However, specific elaboration is required so that states understand the degree of intervention necessary before a formal assessment for special education. IDEA 97 also allows for the expenditure of federal funds to provide incidental support to non-disabled students experiencing the need for similar interventions in the regular classroom setting. This component will need to be expanded so that states can benefit from a broader range of student interventions regardless of the origins of individual teacher/specialist funding sources.

It is not the intent to continue to provide interventions as a method to stall the inevitable assessment of a student who continues to experience school failure. The purpose of the interventions is to prevent the student from developing further failings and gain from the core curriculum with modifications. An 8-12 week period provides a realistic view of the student's ability to benefit from specific instruction that is targeted to those areas of weaknesses in the academic core curriculum of student performance. Should the student require additional intervention because of minimal effect, or if the interventions do not appear to be making a substantial difference in the student's performance ability, then a referral to the Student Success Assessment Team is necessary so that no time is lost in assuring that the student receives appropriate educational services.

RECOMMENDATIONS:

1. SLD eligibility must prescribe specific early interventions for a period of 8-12 weeks at first signs of academic failure.

2. State and federal laws pertaining to special education eligibility must be aligned to allow for maximum front-loading of prevention and intervention strategies prior to referral.

3. The commingling of resources and teaching expertise at the school site must be conjoined for the benefit of all student need regardless of funding source origination.

David W. Gordon
Subcommittee on Education Reform
Washington, D.C., June 6, 2002

Table of Indexes

Lightning Source UK Ltd.
Milton Keynes UK
UKOW04f0718260617
304104UK00007B/525/P

9 781240 471300